LESBIAN SACRED SEXUALITY

LESBIAN SACRED SEXUALITY

TEXT BY
DIANE MARIECHILD

PHOTOGRAPHY BY
MARCELINA MARTIN

WINGBOW PRESS, OAKLAND, CALIFORNIA

Wingbow Press books are published and distributed by Bookpeople, 7900 Edgewater Drive, Oakland, California 94621.
Manufactured in Hong Kong.
Design: Denice M. Dearing, Taos, New Mexico.
Printing: Snow Lion Graphics/SLG Books, Berkeley–Hong Kong.
Library of Congress Catalog Number 94-4125
ISBN 0–914728–83–0

"Pleasures" by Diane Hugs was previously published in *With the Power of Each Breath: A Disabled Woman's Anthology*, published by Cleis Press, copyright © 1985; in *My Story's On! Ordinary Women, Extraordinary Lives*, published by Common Differences Press; in *Lesbian Ethics*, published by Institute of Lesbian Studies, copyright © 1988. "The experience which led me to write `Pleasures' was life altering. Now I know there is so much more, why would I settle for less?"

"letters to kate" from *Letters to Kate* by Joan Iten Sutherland.

"Since Sappho" and "Show Me the Pictures Again" are from *Past, Present & Future Passions* by Barbara Ruth, to be sold to and shared with women only. It is available from Her Books, P.O. Box 7467, Santa Cruz, CA 95061.

Elsa Gidlow poems printed by permission of Druid Heights Artists Retreat.

Material from *Another Mother Tongue* by Judith Grahn, copyright © 1984 by Judith Grahn. Reprinted by permission of Beacon Press.

Material from *Same Sex Love*, edited by Robert H. Hopcke, Karin Loftus Carrington and Scott Wirth, copyright © 1993 by Robert H. Hopcke. Reprinted by arrangement with Shambhala Publications, Inc., 300 Massachusetts Avenue, Boston, MA 02115.

Sue Silvermarie poems quoted are from book–on–tape *Menopausal Lust* available from Silvermarie Productions, 1045 S. 28th, Milwaukee, WI 53215.

"O Honeysuckle Woman," "Close Your Eyes," "Double Phoenix," and "Let Me Touch" by Chrystos reprinted with permission of the author and the publisher, from *Not Vanishing* (Vancouver, Press Gang Publishers, 1988).

"a mother's orgasm at the beginning of her day" by Jeanne Jullion printed by permission of the author.

Excerpts from "Meeting the Tiger" from *Snake Power* reprinted by permission of Sandy Boucher.

First printing March 1995

For Barbara, beloved spiritual partner
—Diane

To the Spirit of Elsa Gidlow 1898–1986 Poet–Warrior
—Marcelina

CONTENTS

ix

INTRODUCTION TO THE PHOTOGRAPHS

I nestle into the body of our Sacred Earth
The wisdom of marsh and sand enters me
I swim silently through the dark, winding waters of the Ogeechee
The sky opens to reveal a universe without time
All this in one moment of touching your body
All this in one moment of breathing your breath
Suddenly I am alone with the Divine

Marcelina Martin

The mystery of life unfolds with wild unpredictability. At any moment I might be swept into a reverie of oneness or into an abyss of despair. Each state of being passes in its own time, yet I am held by the awareness of that streaming force. As an artist I focus on reflecting those moments when the mystery opens and on portraying our relationships within its vastness. I explore the inner visions and myths of people's lives in a process I have named *photomythology*.

Photomythology evolved from the observation that America is primarily a visually oriented culture. The way we perceive reality is influenced by a complex range of imagery. Heroes and myths are intricately woven into our psyches. Our ideas of individual identity, social place, and interrelatedness coalesce from this matrix of images. Some of the most adverse effects of this visual information are submerged in the unconscious, leaving us adrift, unaware that we are in its undertow. As women in a sexist culture we are especially vulnerable to manipulation through imagery. Over thousands of years, our own authentic experiences of womanhood have been erased from the public domain and replaced by fabrications designed for exploitation.

Even if we consciously reject negative images, their power can influence us subconsciously unless we change them at a deep level. If not brought to light and examined, our images evolve into private and eventually public myths and standards. Images we hold are the foundation for the content and action of our lives. Through inquiry into our inner imagery, we can expose outdated myths, produce life-affirming images, and cultivate a dynamic vision of wholeness. In consciously creating our imagery and mythologies, we affect our political, economic, and social attitudes which inspire change in the outer world as well as our inner worlds.

American culture does not hold sacred our bodies or our sexuality. The web of negativity and confusion around sexuality obscures the true nature of sex as sacred connection between human beings. Patriarchal religions have contributed greatly to perverted views about sexuality. The patriarchal need for dominance and power has developed into a pattern of sexual violence. Thus, a disregard for life has arisen. While it is uncomfortable for us to see people showing love or affection publicly, it has become increasingly less disturbing to see anger, violence, and hatred. Actions of kindness and decency have been replaced with acts of aggression and disrespect. Intimacy is viewed as something to hide. Our shame about sexual expression is camouflaged by our belief that sexual matters should be private. In this one word, "private," we hold closely to our discomfort and guilt at feeling the most powerful, beautiful, and exuberant human expression.

The dominant view of sexuality in our society is anti-erotic. The power of sexuality is ceaselessly exploited in advertising. We are constantly overwhelmed by images that reinforce how the physical has been separated from the emotional/psychic/spiritual; how sexuality has been separated from the grace of the sacred whole. This separation from nature has led to a loss of integrity that manifests in our alienation from each other as well as from the Earth.

Restoring the erotic as wholesome is difficult because it has been distorted through power-over interactions, violence as sex, and lust without reverence. There are many sex-negative attitudes in straight gay, and lesbian culture. This fear of one's own sensuality is deeply rooted in misogyny. Reclaiming our erotic nature as vital life force is a political act. We are breaking the rules. To experience dynamic relatedness and to integrate one's sexuality and spirituality are huge contributions to the evolution of life-affirming consciousness. In cherishing and nurturing our bodies and spirits, our connection to each other and the Earth grows.

Mindfulness about our true attitudes towards ourselves and our sexuality is particularly essential for the lesbian community. We have endured many kinds of oppression, but hatred has focused mainly on our sexuality. Most of us have not escaped internalized homophobia. In order to transform these injurious images and feelings, we must ferret out and replace the negative with the life-affirming. By imaging ourselves as whole in our own visual language, we dissolve the prevalent, spurious definitions of our lives. Making contact with the sacred and committing our sexuality to the realm of spiritual practice is the primary focus of *Lesbian Sacred Sexuality*. We can imbue every aspect of our lives with our love and devotion to the sacred and to wholeness. To experience the interconnectedness of all life, our perception of Eros, or self-preservation, is changed forever. Developing this state of reverence towards all life is a great contribution towards preserving and healing our planet. I pray for *Lesbian Sacred Sexuality* to awaken an attitude of respect, if not acceptance, for lesbians.

For a long time I searched for a book that exemplified the spiritual nature of sexuality between women. I have read many Tantric books, but they have all been directed towards the heterosexual experience. The reality of balancing the feminine and the masculine within one gender is never truly accepted. If it was, then the fact that this integration exists in homosexual relationships would be an equally explored avenue of Tantric sexuality. When I decided to create *Lesbian Sacred Sexuality*, I envisioned a book that would allow the reader to go deeply into the connection between sexuality, body, and nature. I thought of the images as an invitation to experience the sacred. I am not attempting to define what is sacred, but rather to give images that may move you deeper into dialogue with yourself. Only you know what is sacred to you. Each person creates a journey towards wholeness. It is not for anyone else to judge whether it is the "right" path. If you do not see your sacred sexuality in this book,

please use these images as a springboard to begin making your own photographs. That is the object of *photomythology*: creating images to embody one's own reality. I hope that readers other than lesbians will find this book of value. After all, we are speaking to the sacredness of all sexuality.

This collaboration began as an exploration of sacredness of our sexuality. Diane and I started with some of our own ideas and moved to shaping a book from these ideas and those that we collected from other women. Most of these were the women who participated in the photographic sessions. In gathering information on how lesbians defined sacred sexuality and setting up the photographic sessions for *Lesbian Sacred Sexuality*, Diane and I had a long conversation with each participant. We entered realms of conversation that few explore. What is *sacred sexuality*? How does the Spirit manifest in your lovemaking? How do you experience the divine in your sexuality? When do you find yourself open to expanded states of consciousness? What kind of mystical experiences have you had while making love? Diane recorded, transcribed, and edited the conversations with the women. In most instances excerpts from the conversations precede the images from that particular session. In a few instances the women's quotes have been integrated into the text. You will find similar ideas and experiences of sacred sexuality echoed throughout the book.

In order to find a way as a photographer to create a visual image of something that is basically unseen, I explored with each participant various images she associated with the feelings and sensations experienced in sacred sexuality. I follow two precepts in my photography: intrude on no one and take only what is given. In keeping with these guidelines, I did not ask to photograph explicit sexual contact. I aligned myself with a certain primal, elemental state of being and focused on entering a heart-centered, holy space with the women. I concentrated on evoking an intimate connection between women and the creative matrix and on presenting a vision of being grounded completely in one's body. My Buddhist practice gave me the equanimity to photograph such profoundly personal moments between women. Through meditation I have learned to practice being only in this moment. This enabled me to give each participant my entire attention and to hold ground for deep intimacy as well as deep pain. Feeling the interconnectedness of all life, I could act as both a personal and an impersonal witness. I say this because many people have asked what it was like to make these photographs. Their first thoughts seem to come directly from the patriarchal ideas associated with pornography. I see this as a conditioned response to the erotic, to see sexuality as fragmented and separated from the Sacred Wholeness of life. My intention with these images is to honor sex as connected to, not separate from, everything else.

Lesbian Sacred Sexuality was a personal journey for both Diane and me. Our search for a meaningful format took us in many directions, including our own sexuality and wounded selves. In photographing such intimacy between others, I recalled my own memories of sacred moments. I remembered how opening myself to the wildness of the heart is offering myself also to the fierceness of love. In yielding, I have experienced bliss and terror; for giving everything is accepting the possibility of losing one's self. This emptiness of no-self can bring a higher state of integration by going through love's journey. The broken heart is a great teacher; the mended heart, an extraordinary healing.

Each photographic session was unique, and each woman contributed her particular energy and courage to this project. Creating a book like Lesbian Sacred Sexuality was not without moments of grave doubt. We were all aware of the hatred and ignorance in our society, and we all were committed towards social change that addresses these problems. With each participant, there was a gulf to cross in grappling with public opinion. I salute all of the women who have been able to find the courage necessary to bring you these images. I particularly want to honor the women whose images were not included in the book. Their participation, none the less, helped to create the book. In this respect, the book is truly a celebration of sexuality and reverence for our bodies.

There was one session in particular when Diane and I felt that we had arrived at the core of this work, the essence of sacred sexuality. On a clear, warm day in September, Diane, Weed, Victoria, and I drove north out of San Francisco to four hundred acres of private land above the Pacific Ocean. We followed a stream into the wilderness of the steep hills beyond Salt Point. Even in a four-wheel drive vehicle, I began to feel nervous about the disappearing road and the wheels edging ever closer to the hundred-foot cliff. As we moved farther into the forest, mankind's abuses of our sacred Earth seemed to drop away. The air turned golden, the birds seemed to sing louder, and a fragrance from the soil and trees rose to embrace us. We began to drive through a series of locked gates. I was reminded of Inanna's descent to the underworld. Clearly this was the journey we were undertaking.

Eventually we arrived at the headwaters of the stream. Giant log jams created incredible sculptures; the Douglas firs stood over us with great majesty. As Diane said, "I intuited that this trip was going to be a particularly important session for us. The journey down the road felt symbolic to me also. We were there for three hours, and it could have been three minutes or three days. I felt safe and held by this land, the elements and the spirits. We had stepped into another realm that was vitally alive."

We soon found our spot, made a prayer circle, and opened to the sacrament of Nature. This land was exceptionally clear and intact. Weed and Victoria's energy together was so profoundly pure. I came into contact with my own wildness again. I felt that unconditional love poured forth around us; the sense of separation from each other, ourselves, and the Earth was gone. In this blessed place, a long-awaited healing happened to me: one which followed four years of Chronic Fatigue Immune Dysfunction Syndrome. This devastating loss of health had taken away the most basic experience of peace in my body. Here, at the headstream of some little-known river, I felt whole and filled with the sweet sense of health that had eluded me. I entered the power of the Sacred. To feel molecules of yourself swirling irretrievably into another, human or tree, opens the door to the nature of the real world. We all touched this primordial ground of being. We all became aware of a numinous quality with which everything glowed—four women, trees, rocks, creek, ferns, sunlight. This was the experience of Sacred Sexuality. We had come into contact with the Universal Source. The strength of wholeness filled all our spirits that afternoon.

May you be blessed with a wholesome sense of the sexual/spiritual connection. May you come into deep union with the Source of life.

Marcelina Martin
Point Reyes, California
Vernal Equinox, 1994

INTRODUCTION TO THE TEXT

*L*esbian Sacred Sexuality is an opportunity for lesbians to reflect on our intimate, sexual and sensual experiences as sacred, whether alone or with a partner. We have included both our own experiences and those of the women who were photographed. We trust that both the similarities and the differences will invoke a profound sense of joy and respect. We can only make suggestions that invite exploration. We invite you to a wise and continuous opening to the Sacred, to consider your intimate and sexual times as opportunities to be in communion with the web of life. This work may summon you to something alive, creative, and vibrant within yourselves and within your relationships to your partners and to creation itself. It may inspire you, and touch some inner chord that will engage you more wholly in your life journey.

Sexuality is at the core of our physical, mental, and emotional nature. Playing with our sexual energy lets us touch another reality or realm, the spiritual or sacred energy that nourishes our physical lives. Awakened sexuality means being fully present in the moment. The book centers on opening to the Sacred through three connections: to our breath, to our bodies, and to the body of the Earth. The focus is to become grounded in our bodies and to feel a genuine appreciation for them as they are *now*. It is to become fully connected to our own energy, the energy of our partner, and the energy of the Earth. In lesbian lovemaking the roles we assume are easily interchangeable. Orgasm isn't always the goal. The experience is one of being totally connected, awake, and alive in this state of vibrant, loving, erotic energy.

I believe that because of its sensuous, total body expression, much of lesbian sexuality might be labeled tantric or contemplative sex. The word *tantra* means continuation, thread or link. Nothing can exist separately, in and of itself. Everything exists in relationship to everything else. To employ tantric methods is to employ the tools that enable this awareness to arise within us, not as intellectual knowledge but as direct, immediate perception of a universal truth. Everything in life, including sex, is embraced and utilized as energy that can be transmuted into the pure essence from which all phenomena in the universe are created.

Our sexuality, like all things in this world, is more fluid than we often realize. Marcelina knew at a very young age that she was "different" and considered herself a lesbian at the age of thirteen. I was in a heterosexual marriage for seven years and had two sons in that marriage before coming out as a lesbian at age thirty. In the spirit of the book, which is celebration and deep exploration, we invite you to explore your sexuality in a gentle, open–hearted way.

This work is presented through the eyes and hearts of two lesbians in midlife. I am a second-generation Italian-American born and raised on the East Coast. Marcelina is a southerner of French/Irish/Cherokee descent. As women who are lovers of women we wanted to celebrate this love. This book grew out of our shared values: respect for ourselves and for all of life, mindfulness of our thoughts, feelings, and actions, as well as a great love for and experience of the complete interconnectedness of nature. Marcelina and I created a process of asking questions and speaking of aspects of sexuality that most people never talk about in depth. The book combines photographs, poetry, prose, comments by participants, journal entries, guided meditations, and energy exercises.

Lesbian Sacred Sexuality is one step on a long journey of unfolding the Sacred in our lives. To recognize the Sacred is to make holy, to make whole. To recognize the Sacred is to see the connection with the divine, to know that we are divine. We acknowledge the Sacred by treating all of life with respect and reverence. When we recognize the Sacred, this attitude informs everything that we do; thus our thoughts, words, and actions are transformed. Experiencing life as sacred allows us to slow down and greet each person and each of life's circumstances in a more gentle way. When we revere each person, each object, each situation, we treat them with loving care. When we rush or when we are afraid or angry, we often do harm. Connected to and part of the divine, the whole, the holy, we respond to everyone, including ourselves, with kindness, clarity, and compassion.

Often, because of the pain we have experienced at the hands of people attached to religious dogma, we have a distrust of the spiritual. We confuse the true spirit of life with limiting and negative belief systems. It is important to make a clear distinction between the sacred spiritual realm and the religious doctrines of the dominant culture. The recognition of the Sacred is an attitude, a way of being in the world.

The images and metaphors we use to talk about the Sacred are culturally conditioned. Each of us has her own racial and cultural identity which informs how we express it. Many of us have a particular religious tradition into which we were born and often a different one that we have chosen or created. I have had visionary experiences during lovemaking, and the images that arose were colored both by my family's religious tradition and the spiritual traditions I have studied and practiced over the years.

The joy and the wonder of the Sacred is in its vastness. Ritual and imagery provide a doorway to the sacred for many of us. Each of us needs to find her own way of expressing the divine, to discover and generate symbols, concepts, and models that express her spiritual vision. The Pele meditation and two journal entries that include a specific Goddess serve as an invitation for you to enter the more subtle layers of your own experience.

Opening to the Sacred is often a transformative process. Whatever prevents us from a direct experience of the Sacred must be transformed. For this reason we have discussed the shadow in intimate relationships, exploring desire from a spiritual perspective and moving from the personal to the universal.

Western culture is primarily focused on the external world. Finding words to describe an inner experience is challenging. A poem's image can recall for us something we always knew, yet never articulated. We have included several meditations and exercises working with the breath. It is only through close, intimate contact with the breath, our life essence, that we can have close, intimate contact with another person. "Pele's Breath" and "Meditation" are exercises to work with alone as support for becoming centered and grounded. "Love's Energy" and "Contemplative Sex" are exercises that can be done with a partner or adapted for an individual.

The women who were photographed range in age from twenty–five to fifty–eight and include lesbians of African-American, Caribbean, European-American, Japanese, and Spanish-American heritage. They were photographed in a variety of settings including their own homes, the studio, and nature. Opening to the sacredness of all creation is sensing our profound ties with nature and with all beings. Crystal, Hallie, and many of the women photographed spoke of their closeness to nature, of making love in nature and of feeling part of the whole web of life. Antonia and Patti each described sexual experiences that became a means for greater self–knowledge and expression as well as a vehicle to travel in other dimensions. Beth, whose name in Hebrew means *temple*, spoke of sex as worship; for Wolf, lovemaking was a sacred dance.

Opening to the Sacred is opening to the sanctity of our own bodies, loving our bodies, being fully present and free from self–consciousness. Judith, one of the women photographed, talked of the powerfully erotic sense she experiences as a large woman making love with a woman larger than herself. Berjé spoke of reclaiming her identity when she became lovers with another woman of color. Nancy, a woman living with AIDS, shared how her partner's tenderness and their lovemaking transformed her negative feelings of being poison.

Opening to the Sacred is a healing experience. Terri, an abuse survivor, spoke of the healing power of sex as she reclaimed lost parts of herself. Cindy, one of my friends who is an incest survivor, noticed over the years the positive effect her body meditation practice had on her ability to experience sexual pleasure.

Lesbian Sacred Sexuality is a beginning exploration of sacred sexuality. Many of us consider our sexuality and our lovemaking as sacred. Others may sense the specialness but have not yet considered sexuality or ourselves as sacred. Some of us may have experienced a healing through lovemaking but have not looked at sexuality as a doorway into the spiritual realm. There is no one place we need to be. All we need to do is begin to celebrate and explore where we are right at this moment.

May the sacred flame of love be rekindled in your hearts and bellies.
May you know your power and beauty.
May the heat of your sacred lovemaking bring blessings to the world.

Diane Mariechild
Blue Moon, 1993

LESBIAN SACRED SEXUALITY

INVOCATION TO SAPPHO

Sappho
      Sister–Mother
              free–
souled, fire–hearted
Psappha of Mitylene on
sea–lapped Lesbos
miracle of a woman
           (Strabo wrote)
now   now
        let me declare
devotion.
Not light years   love years
on how many love years
across fields of the dead
does your fragrance
travel to me?

Since maidenhood in brain   blood
by you haunted
in my own armpits I have breathed
sweat of your passion
in the burning crotch of the lover
tasted your honey
heard   felt in my pulse
            day long
               night through
lure of your song's beat
insistently echo.

By dust of five–and–twenty centuries
                not smothered
by book–consuming flames of
the hate–filled churchmen
             unsilenced
your fame only haloed   made
more splendid.

Sappho, little and dark,
the Beautiful, Plato called you
(though his Republic had
grudging use for poets)
Sappho whose veins ran fire
           whose nerves
quivered to loves illicit now
            in your day
honored by the noblest,
Sappho, all roses,
Do we not touch
across the censorious years?

Elsa Gidlow, 1965

LESBIAN SACRED SEXUALITY

Erotic love between women can be a celebration of and an initiation into the female creative spirit, the feminine mysteries. When we open to the great feminine, the holy space that is the foundation of the world, making love becomes sacred. Lesbians hold the form of woman power at its most profound. Many lesbians seek to identify ourselves from an inner source of woman wisdom. With each act of loving we can embrace this deep inner space and explore the possibility of returning to our original perfection. Woman loving woman can be an alchemical process which reaches into our very cells. Through the purity of this energy we may recognize the essential wholeness of nature. We know ourselves as "virgin," meaning one–in–herself, belonging to no man. Lesbian sacred sexual love has the potential to awaken and reunite us with the divine source of our being. Whether or not we have sexual partners depends on many factors, including our circumstances, our karma* and our life purpose. Sex is sex. It is not our partner's gender that makes our sex sacred. It is the consciousness that we bring to our sexual acts that makes them sacred, whether we are making love to ourselves or with a partner. Lesbian love is sacred when it is visionary, interconnected, and transformational. Through the power of love we come to know ourselves as both mothers/creators of our lives and as daughters/caretakers of the Earth. Our lives and our work can become expressions of this wisdom and power.

*Karma is a Sanskrit word whose meaning is *action*: the working of cause and effect whereby positive actions produce happiness and negative actions produce suffering.

INITIATION

From womb to womb, connection clear and strong. My body sits upon the Earth, my heart energy streams down into the core of the Earth. Her energy like the waters of a mighty river flows through me. My body opens, my blood becomes like sparkling water fed from a boundless source springing from the heart of the Earth. My light body* full and shimmering gently withdraws from my physical body and melts through a crack, thus entering sacred ground.

My body pulses with the Earth, hot and dry, yet fed by unseen waters. Three eagles soar above, spirit friends bringing me to the land of the endless sky. I walk through this land for a long time until a holy space beckons me. I descend into that dark, round space. My eyes can see nothing, then gradually changing forms dimly appear. Who enters this space with me? Lovers of the past, friends from all the cycles of my life, each of us on her private journey. Here together in this sacred place.

Sounds of a drum rise through the darkness. I circle and leap to its beat, leaving the heaviness behind. Only the sacred child dances within the holy round. My body lighter and lighter, joy bubbling forth and encircling this sacred space. Abruptly the drumming stops. The echoes die. Silence settles on me like the fog that slides down the mountain and fills the valley I call home. My body fills with energy: full, deep, and clear. No buzz of expectation. Strong, open, and spacious. As my eyes become accustomed to the dark I see the circle: sisters of fire, women through the ages, young and old, of every race and tradition.

One crone, strong and stately, approaches me. We stand face to face. Her face is dark and lined with age. Her eyes hold mine in a steady, welcoming gaze. As I drink in her beauty she begins to transform before me, her lined skin becoming smooth and then

* The light body, also called the inner, astral, or energy body, permeates and is enveloped by the physical body.

wrinkling and softening again. She is Mother of the Flame, a firekeeper from the beginning. She raises her hand in greeting and a tiny fire flickers, then blazes on her palm. She touches my belly, heart, and head, belly, heart, and head. The third time she touches me, her hand strokes my yoni and remains there for moments until she enters me. A sound breaks the stillness, the sound of fire igniting. I feel its warmth spread through my yoni, my pelvis. Belly bowl holds this fire, contains its power, as the flames dance higher. My heart burns, tiny fingers of flame pierce its walls and it becomes open space, the endless sky. My eyes sparkle as the fire dances through my mind, its flames licking away my fears. Burned away. Burned away. Burned away.

I know without words: This is initiation. Lesbian lovemaking is a celebration and initiation into the holy space that is the foundation of the world. I step back and bow low. The drums start. A muffled steady beat grows louder and stronger. We circle around, moving to the rhythm. Vibrations bounce off the walls, rising and falling back to the Earth. Energy spirals upward, filling my legs as they stretch down into the Earth. My strong legs like columns, my pelvis the arch cradling my sacred inner place. Earth energy flows upward to legs, through pelvis and back to Earth. My bones become the soil, my flesh becomes the Earth. The drums call us from deep in the heart of the Earth. Womanspirits, ancestors, grandmothers of time, we dance. The snakes that lay coiled in baskets around the room begin to stir. I feel the energy rise along my spine. I am flying, down in that holy round, lightly touching the ground. I am flying. And I am touching holy ground.

The drums stop. The sisters of fire become shadows on the wall. Then total darkness. My belly, my heart, my mind cast a soft glow. The fire within, now banked, will warm and nourish me. I climb up the ladder, slowly, gratefully. I touch the Earth. I bow to the endless sky.

FEMALE SEXUAL POWER

Rarely do the books, from translations of ancient texts to modern sex manuals, speak of sex between same-sex partners as sacred. Whether referring to Hindu tantric practices or Chinese sexual yoga, most of the techniques described are directed towards heterosexual couples. We are told the man holds the yang and the woman the yin, and, through their sexual union, the energy is balanced. Yet each of us, woman or man, contains both the yin and the yang energy. They are the rivers of life that spiral upward through the spine. It is not necessary to have sexual union with the opposite sex to balance us. The wholeness that is spoken of in all spiritual traditions is the openness of the heart. It is finding the balance of sacred life energy within each human being. For this balance to be possible we must first love and accept ourselves. In finding this balance we move beyond our personal boundaries to a communion with all life.

The female power of the serpent curling out of the womb has everything to do with sex and nothing to do with it. It is the symbol of the material world—that which can be touched—infused with spirit, embodying spirit as the ocean is permeated by salt. It is the symbol of procreation-creation–the power to make, make new–the primordial rising up of life once more, and yet again, in all settings and against all odds. It speaks of the coming-together and the falling-apart that make our life/death, light/dark, hope/despair; yet it is a continuous round of creation–its only urge: to be. Sandy Boucher

In patriarchal society, women are seen as sexual objects, to be bought and possessed. We are taught that our bodies are shameful. We are abused. We don't know how to be truly intimate and, while sexual activity can be intimate, it is often not, given the power–over dynamics and woman–hating that are inbred in our culture. Lack of education, negative feelings about bodily functions, woman–hating, and the high incidence of childhood sexual abuse have created fear and shame around sex and sexuality. Confusion and guilt about sexuality create limiting ideas such as the belief that the only purpose of sex is to reproduce.

We know that lesbian lovemaking does not produce children. It is for pleasure, warmth, emotional and sensual connection, and can be a doorway into experiencing the divine. The energy exchanged in sacred sex can be healing on an emotional and physical level. People who believe that sex is dirty or solely for reproduction often consider lesbian sex abnormal and sinful. People who cling to this way of thinking feel justified in their repression, discrimination, and harassment of lesbians. Lesbians often internalize these attitudes and suffer with painful feelings of guilt, self–hatred, and denial.

To be able to know we're lesbians in a world where we're bombarded with heterosexual messages and expectations, means we have been listening to a strong, inner voice. Cindy

SHAMELESS

Your fire, your scent.
Your presence, your juices.
With me. In me.
Part of me.
Above, below, all around me:
Your beauty!
This passion,
wakes me up
to a different country!
Here I can do nothing
but surrender.

Kissing you, I'm still kissing you
though you are flying away.

A river rushes in my body,
love runs and floods,
offers up from its riverbed,
gleaming for each of us,
treasure upon treasure.
Wet. Fierce. Softened.
My cunt opens to you
across a continent of flying.
Shameless. Shameless.

Sue Silvermarie

PATTI & BETH

I have two kinds of sexual experiences that I feel are sacred. The first experience happens when I feel very connected with Beth and there is a strong feeling of love between us. That is the most intense part. The touching, even subtle touching is also intense, but it is not at all goal–oriented towards orgasm. It might not even involve touching clits for a long time. It is a whole body experience, where every part of the body is as important as every other part. Fingers, hands, face, arms, thighs, feet, breasts, all feel as good as the genitals. It is transcendent in that I feel connected to Beth and connected to everything through a sense of love. My heart is very open and my body is alive, but the actual sexual touching is not what is important. Sexual touching may happen at the end to release some of the energy but that is not the goal. I've named this type of lovemaking "exquisite sex."

The other kind of sacred sexual experience happens when I feel open, trusting, and present. The sexual energy is a vehicle for going to another place in my consciousness. It is more centered in the body and there is sexual stimulation combined with the trust in my partner that allows me to go to another dimension. I call this "cosmic sex." Sometimes if we're making love outdoors I look up at the sky and feel like I'm a bird, flying. Or I have visual experiences, mostly of nature. Beth is not experiencing what I am experiencing at the moment. She is helping me go there. I talk to her and describe what I'm experiencing because I want Beth to go there with me. I feel like I'm vibrating and I'm taking off into the cosmos. I've had this vibrating feeling without sex, too. It has happened during meditation or in a room filled with people chanting. There is a lot of energy and it starts flowing through me like an electrical current. This kind of experience is like a window or doorway opening into another world, another way of being, which reminds me that everything divine exists inside of me.

When Patti and I were first making love we called it worshipping; worshipping the other person, her body, her spirit, her soul. We both got off on my name, which in Hebrew means house of worship. Patti called it worshipping at the temple of Beth. That is how I feel when we're making love. Sex has really changed for me over the years. It is a much more spiritual act for me now. I had always experienced wonderful passion and heightened experiences, junk food sex, and a whole variety of experiences but now I feel that I reach a much deeper level. Lovemaking is now more of a spiritual practice where in the past it was an addiction for me.

The frequency and the quality seem to be inversely proportional to one another. Patti and I don't make love nearly as often as we did during our courtship; however, the quality is incomparable. I don't have the same sexual appetite. I had lots of big open needs that were filled with sex and love from a variety of sources. I had many lovers and it seemed to work for me at the time. It wasn't very thoughtful or intentional, it was just the way things worked then. I don't judge it. It wasn't bad, it's just that this has shifted for me now. The quality of lovemaking has changed for me. I wouldn't impose monogamy or the idea that "less is more" on anyone else, but from my personal experience, less is more. My relationship with Patti (as well as my relationship to myself and to "the great spirit") is profoundly different. There is a sense of security and calmness. The love is always there and doesn't have to be sought necessarily through a sexual act. I woke up this morning feeling penetrated and permeated by this abundance of love which exists for me now on so many subtle planes.

What is different for me now in lovemaking is that I often cry from my core. I cry about seventy–five percent of the time we make love. It is feeling love on a really deep level and it just wells up from inside and I cry. It is like an emotional orgasm. It has very little to do with the physical orgasm, although that happens too. This orgasm feels similar in form to the physical kind, it has a wavelike form but it comes from a different place. It touches the essence of my being. I feel incredibly nurtured and feel vibration throughout my whole being. I tend to be a scientific type person, focused on and distracted by the outer world. This new form of sexuality is like a mantra in meditation, it is a spiritual practice.

14

15

DANCE OF INTIMACY

Sometimes now I watch younger people cruising and making out, and I remember the great engine of lust that used to propel me. And the many ways I used sex—with partners male and female—over the years. To express love and tenderness, for entertainment, in order to relax, to avoid something that was bothering me, to be reassured, to prove to myself that I was desirable, to make a conquest, i.e., to get someone to pay attention to me, open to me, "surrender" to me. Sandy Boucher

Learning to love is a process. When we rush madly into relationships, driven by passion, then we lose grounding (our authentic center), and there isn't anything to give. Without patience for ourselves, for each other, and for the process, there can be no love. Intimate relationship must become a dance, an artful movement between respecting our own needs and wants and being open enough to take risks, to become vulnerable and flexible, without getting too personally attached or held down by these needs. We are dancing on the edge of what separates us from a direct experience of the world and, when we slip, we get bruised. We regain our balance by learning to bring awareness to the moments of losing balance.

The practice of mindfulness meditation* assists us in our relationships because it highlights what separates us from a direct experience of the world. We learn to renounce the separations, not the world. We create obstacles by identifying with thoughts and feelings, by trying to grasp the ones we like, and by trying to eliminate those we don't like. With practice we begin to see how the drama of our lives is created by this push and pull. We see the gaps in the constant stream of thoughts and come to know these gaps, this space, as the ultimate reality or ground of being. Prior to this we saw the changing flow of thoughts and feelings as our only reality.

A present-day meditation master has used this analogy. Our thoughts and feelings are like a river. If we try to stop them we will meet resistance. It is better to go with the flow and be aware of everything that enters the river. Watch the birth, duration, and disappearance of every thought, feeling, and sensation. The resistance disappears, the river keeps flowing, only now it is flowing in the sunlight of awareness. Every moment of awareness is a moment of control. Even though the river is still there, we feel peaceful.

*Two basic types of meditation practice: concentration practices which include visualization and mantra (sacred sound) repetition, and awareness or mindfulness practice. Mindfulness practice focuses the attention on a primary object such as the breath, bodily sensations, feelings, or mind states. The attention touches the predominant object lightly and then moves to the next predominant object. For example, from breath, to sound, to sensation in knee, to breath, to thinking, to sound, to breath.

MEDITATION

This meditation uses the sitting posture but it is not necessary to sit in order to meditate. Walking and lying down are also meditation postures. If physical conditions prevent you from sitting, please lie down. I spent three months on meditation retreat using primarily the lying–down posture because of arthritis in my spine. Of course, it is easier to fall asleep this way, so although sleepiness and restlessness are present at different times, there is more sleepiness than restlessness when lying down. In the sitting posture there is often more restlessness. I have found it useful to make an audio tape of guided meditations or have a friend read them to me.

Sit in a comfortable position with your spine held erect. Make sure that your neck and head are neither jutting forward nor drooping backward. If you are sitting in a cross–legged position be sure that your knees are lower then your hips. Place folded blankets under your knees if they don't touch the floor. Allow your hands to rest in your lap. You may want to cradle your left hand in your right hand with your thumbs lightly touching. Close your eyes or leave them open and downcast, focusing on a point beyond the tip of your nose.

Make no attempt to create any images or to get rid of thoughts or images. Let the breath be your focus of attention. Welcome your attention to the place in your body where you sense or feel your breath most strongly. It may be the base of your nostrils or the belly or chest. Watch your breath as it moves in and out of your body. When thoughts, feelings, or images arise, notice them and gently bring your attention back to the breath. Keep repeating this process without making judgments or either clinging to feelings or pushing them away.

Sit quietly and keep inviting your attention back to the breath. When thoughts arise, notice the thoughts without either following or attempting to repress them. Come back to the breath. Return to the breath whenever you realize your mind has wandered. Know that you are breathing. Know that you are seated on the earth and the sky is above you. You are breathing. Trust the breath. Allow the breath. Welcome the breath throughout your whole being. Breathe.

When the meditation is completed, acknowledge once again that you are sitting and breathing. You may want to make a small bow. Then slowly stand.

SEX, DEATH, AND MEDITATION

I break through
the membrane of earth.
Stars greet me
as a piece of light.
I dart exuberant,
a wisp of fire,
part of a star.
The depths of space,
of grander dimension
than I had imagined.
Enough room, finally,
for my true size.

Exultant,
all alive,
I hear stars
singing like whales
in the galactic sea.
This black womb
cradles me.
Acupoints
meridian the Milky Way
with starfire.

How can I hold such luminosity?
I fall back
toward the atmosphere of earth.
Fall fast
back to my disguise.

Sue Silvermarie

JOURNAL ENTRY, August 2

I woke Saturday morning feeling intense sexual desire. My partner did not want to make love and I chose not to make love to myself. I went into my study and sat down in the rocking chair near my altar. I began to silently chant a mantra. I imagined myself back in a cave in Katmandu. I had repeated the mantra about three times when a vision of a Goddess seated on a lotus throne with a consort appeared in the air above and in front of my head. I was both watching and engaging in the vision at the same time. I knew myself to be one and the same as the consort. The Goddess stepped off the throne and began making love to me. The body of light entered my body fully. Then the Goddess assumed a seated posture and I sat on her lap. I felt great bliss as the Goddess melted into me. My whole being sparkled. I felt the pleasure of our union spread from my yoni throughout my entire body. The Goddess seemed to be saying all my needs would be met, even sexual ones, though no words were spoken. I was safe and protected in a boundless universe. The sexual energy was so powerful and pleasurable I realized that I had experienced a union or complete integration of the yin and yang energies within myself.

The delightful sensations continued and The Blue Tara* immediately appeared and began caressing me. She had a lovely lilting laugh. She wrapped her arms around me and covered me with kisses and lotus blossoms. Next the twenty–one Taras appeared, each more beautiful then the other. All smiles and laughter, they kissed my eyes, my lips, my throat, my breasts, my vulva, my feet. We were floating in the sky, rolling and laughing. Tara's kisses were the softest and most penetrating kisses I have ever experienced. We were dakinis** dancing and making love in the sky. Every cell in my body seemed to shimmer and dance. This whole event happened very quickly and I felt a great ease and delight in my body.

The bliss expanded out into a feeling of great peace which lasted for four days without wavering. There was no tension within my mind. There was no desire for sex or wanting anything outside myself.

I knew without words the meaning of this experience. There are incredible reservoirs of bliss available to us. We do not need a physical partner to experience this. The heart must be open and vulnerable. This powerful experience happened in the moment I both embraced the sensation of desire and let go of grasping, expectation, hope, and fear. In that moment my consciousness opened out into a profound level of energy and depth of understanding.

---

*For Tibetans, Tara is a Buddha (an awakened being). She made and achieved her vow of becoming enlightened in the body of a woman. Tara is the great protector who sits with her right leg slightly extended, ready to step out into the world to offer aid and comfort.

**Dakini, literally translated as *sky–goer*, is the most important manifestation of the feminine in Tibetan Buddhism. Dakinis may appear as human beings or peaceful or wrathful Goddesses, or may be perceived as a play of energy. The dakini represents the everchanging flow of energy with which the yogic practitioner must work in order to become realized.

a mother's orgasm at the beginning of her day

the purity of orgasm
burns me clean
my body extends
into a single spike
of purest pleasure
tears seep
from the corners of my eyes
in acute extended longing
for the land from
whence this comes
how I long for thee and
have my whole life
harbinger of
another world
whose door sucks open
during sex
"I will not be forgetful of thee.
Why, I have carved thy image
in the palms of my hands;
those walls of thine
dwell ever
before my eyes."*

a gigantic hand
rolls the pin of pleasure
over the dough of my belly
pins and yanks my ankles down
twists and pulls my neck up higher
bends down my toes to ballet points
stretches my skin
out of its furrows

*(Isaiah 49:16)

blasts my hair out the
top of a funnel
cries seep from my mouth
in wonder
break from my throat like
boulders
the shell of dailyness and
shards of worry crack
and clatter to the side
the wet body
shot over the ocean
lives for the
moment of firing

what is that I touch
who is that I am
pressed clean through the
vortex of sex
mouth agape
hands loosened
worm of grace in the
earthen sheets
the mother is other now
only she
and soft rolls of thunder
in the distance of her belly
come with her
as she steps
into
her day

Jeanne Jullion

Patti

I woke up in the middle of the night and I couldn't go back to sleep. After doing a number of things like reading, I decided to masturbate because sometimes an orgasm relaxes me and I can go back to sleep. I began making love to myself and started thinking about all the different times in my life when I made love with someone else, when my heart was very open, and I felt extremely connected to the other person, myself and everything in the moment.

I began to make love to myself as if I were that other person. I was making love to myself as if I were someone that I loved and respected, someone to whom I was extremely attracted and felt deeply connected. I made love to myself for over an hour. It was lovemaking on a level different from just sexual. It wasn't goal–oriented. There was a lot of patience, love, and attention, and it could have gone on and on.

The next day I felt the same as if I had been making love all night with a partner. I was in a great mood all day. It was amazing to me that I could really make love with myself, be in love with myself, the way that people think you can do only with another person.

MOVING FROM THE PERSONAL
TO THE UNIVERSAL

Sexual power is potentially so overwhelming that we often deny or trivialize it. We fear this energy because we feel that it is beyond our control. Sexual power is the energetic force that brings forth life on this Earth. Whereas no child is conceived through lesbian lovemaking, the creative life energy can conceive a new attitude, perception, or way of being in the world. When we engage in sexual acts we connect our personal selves with a power greater than ourselves. Our experience and understanding of our sexuality affects our personal lives, our herstory, and the cellular network of relationships that form the basis of life. Standards, values, ideas, and belief systems about sex come primarily from learned or conditioned behavior. These ideas, attitudes, and beliefs have been assimilated into our personalities so that we are not always conscious of them.

We live in a time of awakening consciousness. We are moving from a recognition of the personal, individual self into a transpersonal understanding of the most deep and subtle interconnections of the universe. Bringing mindfulness and consciousness to our lovemaking expands the power of the personal to the transpersonal. This expansion makes possible a healing that resonates through the entire tapestry of the planet. We view ourselves in context with the web of creation. When we experience ourselves within this net of life, then the "I," the "me" is not more important than anything else. There is no longer me and the circumstances outside me; we are part of the whole fabric of the universe.

VICTORIA & WEED

Victoria

Passion can grow and ripen. It can be comfortable and maturing. We have a wonderful life together and I feel blessed. I want to take this spark from our relationship and share it with the lesbian community. That's why I wanted to be photographed for this book. It is the kind of book I wish I could have read when I was coming out.

Weed

Sex is connected with spirituality and consciousness. It isn't just a physical act. Sex has become so materialistic in our culture. Sexuality, when joined with everything in life instead of being fragmented, brings healing. I cry when we make the best love. I don't know why but I think it is healing. I feel it comes from being totally open and trusting.

JILL

Jill

After years of searching for my perfect teacher, I awoke to discover that she was none other than Nature, our Mother, herself. By opening to the Earth's energies and accepting them as my guides, a profound shift occurred in my attitudes towards Her. Later insights showed me that I no longer had to locate the Mother outside myself—that my own body was made up of the same atoms that had been present at the time of the Earth's creation, was pulsing with circulating fluids, had the air of life breathing through it, and was warmed by the fire of its own body heat—held all the Earth's elements I had previously sought outdoors.

As I continue to journey within my own body, I find that there is no barrier between the inner and the outer. Nature is not out there to be called in, but is and always was a part of me. Touching my body sweetly I touch all life. The teacher I seek, the externalized truth I have found in Nature is within me as well. My own sacred body is Her gateway, and only my conditioned mind prevents me from knowing the authentic experience of Her.

29

SACRED SEXUALITY AS DEEP CONNECTION WITH THE UNIVERSE

Sacred sexuality needs neither fancy techniques nor a partner. It flows from an openness to the creative energy of the universe. When we experience the interrelationship of all beings, then who we are–sexually, emotionally, mentally, and physically–is sacred. When I am attuned with creation, I feel energized and at peace. I feel my whole body alive and tingling. I sometimes experience states of arousal that demand no release. It is a sensation of being thrilled to be alive. I can walk on the beach and feel this sense of oneness with the waves, the playful seals, the sun on the water, the breeze on my body. I can rest in this state of arousal while lying in the sand dunes. There is no tension, no need to make love to myself or to anyone else. It is a space of openness and groundedness. I am no longer dwelling in my small self; I am centered within this great universe. It is from this space that sacred sex with another becomes a possibility.

Awareness of ourselves as the Goddess is a gift of grace. Many experiences in my life have filled me with grace: walking in nature, chanting, meditation, mantra recitation, rituals, dance. When I make love to myself or with a partner from this Goddess space, there is more energy to be shared with the universe.

Sacred sexuality or tantric sex is about awareness. It is opening to all the senses without any goal, just openness. The sexual energy arises spontaneously through non–activity. That is, nothing is being done to force it, prolong it, or make it come to some preconceived desired end.

In the conventional way of viewing the world we see things as separate from ourselves and separate from each other. Tantric awareness is a radical understanding of the inherent unity of the universe. Women often have an easier time than men in realizing the connection between our bodies and the body of the planet, the body of the universe. Our moon cycles present us with the direct experience of the ebb and flow of life. There is constant change and yet this changing process is infused with a radical unity. All things, all beings are interconnected. And it is at this level of awareness, of interconnection, that lesbians, women loving women, have much to share about the dynamic dance of love. We have more freedom in changing roles, in experiencing a wider range of behavior and feelings. Our lovemaking is not focused on one single act. Our sexuality can be sacred, playful, lustful, serious, humorous, joyful, tender, angry, or anxious. Our sexual communion becomes tantric when it serves as initiation to the "body" of the universe. Our sexual acts become acts of worship when each partner experiences herself and the other as Goddess/Divine.

Nature is a great healer for me. I feel myself pulled to the mountains. Being close to nature intensifies the sacredness of sex. Crystal

EXPLORING DESIRE FROM A SPIRITUAL PERSPECTIVE

Because we are obsessed with sex (we being all of us as well as American society in general), we think it unfortunate when someone is not "doing it." For myself it is a great relief not to be so motivated by lust. When I was making love a great deal, I did not ask myself about the significance of sex in my life, about how I used it, how I might go about it differently. If I felt desire, I did everything possible to satisfy that desire—without hesitation or reflection, and without regret.

Sandy Boucher

Desire for wholeness is the spark that summons us toward spiritual growth. Even when this yearning or desire is not conscious we have an intuitive sense that wholeness is possible. Often this deep longing arises from a sense of estrangement. We feel separate and alone. As long as this primal longing remains unconscious we may find ourselves addicted to substances or in unhealthy relationships. Becoming conscious of this hunger for reunion can lead us back to a recognition of our inherent wholeness. The power of Lesbian Sacred Sexuality is that it can give us both a vision and an experience of the interconnectedness of life.

Passionate connection can transform our lives. However, transformation can be frightening because it requires us to give up the safety of our habits, our assumptions, our limiting views, or our self–protective stances. We may no longer be able to hide behind comfort and convenience. Transformation or spiritual awakening is a process of deconstruction. We see how we have become identified with concepts, ideas, and feelings. Egotistical perceptions—"I want, I own, I like, I don't like"—keep us bound to a limited vision of the world. As we become aware of each moment during which the mind grasps an idea or feeling and identifies with it, our identification lessens and we awaken to a universal perspective, one of interrelationship.

The awakened state is an honest state. There is no denial of pain and no refusal to accept pleasure. We must risk all the attitudes and prejudices to which we cling without knowing if there will be a return for our efforts. When we can loosen the hold our opinions and prejudices have on us, we can open into the space of universal awareness. We can consciously live from and within the embrace of the Goddess. Knowing that we are the Goddess, that we have the potential to awaken, gives us the strength and the courage to investigate beyond conventional reality. If we live from this Goddess awareness, if we know our self–worth, we can learn to distinguish between the wholesome desire for love and connection and harmful desire/grasping.

Women who have been seriously hurt and carry that pain in their hearts need time to do the work of healing body, mind, and heart. If we don't feel we have the right to be, we must heal this pain before we can gain the understanding we seek. With healing we learn how to nourish and care for ourselves. With healing we learn how to communicate with clarity and sensitivity. When we realize that our capacity for happiness is greater after healing has taken place, we will have the confidence and self–love necessary for continued exploration. If we have an interest in close and detailed observation, we can choose to investigate further.

We all know how it feels when we are open and lovingly connected. We also know how it feels to be contracted and grasping onto someone or something. All of us have probably been harmed by someone reaching for us, not in a loving and connected way but in a grasping way. Most of us have also experienced this painful grasping and contraction within ourselves and we have probably caused harm to others by acting out this grasping. When we examine the nature of desire/grasping, we must look at how we have constructed our personalities. This includes looking at how and what we have identified with: looking at "I" and being able to sometimes put aside what "I" wants and needs. We do this, not from a feeling of scarcity, but from an interest in understanding how we have identified with desire.

The practice of sacred lesbian sex can be a doorway into experiencing ourselves as part of the marvelous web of dancing energy that is life. Many women long for a direct relationship with the source of life. We may have experienced this relationship through dramatic events such as experiencing or witnessing childbirth, listening to great music, swimming in a cool mountain stream, or gathering the first spring flowers.

While dramatic events often create the opening for a wise understanding of the wholeness of life, it is spiritual practice (meditation, contemplation, mindfulness) that enables us to sustain the awareness. For almost two decades I have studied and practiced Buddhist meditation. This practice has had a profound affect on how I view the world. Rather than asking me to believe something because of someone else's experience, Buddhist practice has given me tools for my own deep investigation and observation.

Being a lesbian was good preparation for my Buddhist practice. I had already learned, as many of us have by living in a heterosexist, homophobic culture, to question everything, to take nothing for granted, and to create my own path. In my life, both Buddhism and lesbian feminism have been liberating forces. Concerned with change and transformation, both Buddhism and feminism emphasize individual responsibility and empowerment. Feminism addresses the inequality and pain that exist because of gender discrimination. Buddhism addresses the universal suffering whose root cause is identification with concepts and ideas, believing that sense contacts make happiness. The practices of feminism and Buddhism both create conditions for a living vision of women outside patriarchal definitions.

Sex can be both a common and a dramatic union of self and other. The ordinary experience of sexual pleasure can afford us a momentary glimpse of the bliss that constitutes our ultimate nature. Yet, no matter how intensely satisfying our sexual communion may be, its bliss is limited. The heat of love's fire eventually dissipates and leaves us alone and wanting more. We are physical, sensate beings; our needs and desires (whether expressed or suppressed) are never-ending.

Conventional reality teaches us that happiness comes from fulfilling as many desires, wants, and needs as possible. Spiritual reality teaches that happiness comes from understanding how we've become identified with our desires. Beneath all our actions in the world is a fear of the unpleasant and a desire for the pleasant. This fear is often unconscious, yet it is expressed through a variety of coping methods: We may try to have absolute order and control or we may become people pleasers. We may get angry when things don't go our way, or we may escape into fantasy. We may try to figure everything out intellectually, submit to an authority figure, or madly dash after pleasure. A deep exploration of our desire for pleasant experiences can make these coping methods conscious. The more clearly we see through the coping methods, the less these patterns will control our behavior.

It is important to understand the two levels of truth, the truth of the mundane world and the truth of the spiritual realm that is the foundation of the world. We need to be able to juggle both levels of truth and not be attached to or confused by either. In the ordinary world it is important for us to recognize our socialization as women. We are told that it is wrong to have sexual desires. Our needs are to be sacrificed for the needs of someone else–parent, sibling, friend, co-worker, or partner. The message is strong: Our feelings and desires do not count. Many women have been punished for having desires or needs, sexual or otherwise. Physical and sexual abuse has damaged countless others. As a result, we often suppress our desires. The hard work of feeling good about ourselves, identifying and expressing our feelings and needs is an ongoing healing process for many of us. For those of us who were seriously wounded by abuse, female socialization, gender discrimination, and lesbophobia, entertaining the idea that fulfilling all our desires won't bring happiness seems counter to our healing work.

Each time we explore the feeling of desire, we have an opportunity to uncover the source of the desire. For many of us who have suppressed our desires, a further investigation can show us that pain comes not only from suppression, but from over–identification; we have identified with conditions of scarcity (we are not worthy, we are not good enough, smart enough, attractive enough). If we create a new set of conditions and then over–identify with them, we won't find freedom. Freedom comes from an awareness of the mind's tendency to identify with or grasp onto conditions, whatever they may be.

It is crucial for lesbians not to mistake this understanding of desire and craving with the confusion and self–hatred we sometimes feel around sexuality because of society's denigrating attitudes towards lesbians. There is no need to feel badly about our sexual desires or the habit of desire itself. There is no moral judgment that says to have desire is evil and to be without desire is good. We need to feel good about being alive and being who we are. We can learn to work with the energy of desire. We can learn to identify the difference between desire as loving connection and desire as some mind movement towards grasping, which can cause harm.

Conventional healing methods (even those we label alternative) cannot get at the root of this problem. We can't change the ego with the ego. We must observe the mind, and this is what we do in awareness meditation practice. The process of exploration and observation is a gentle and attentive process. It is tolerant and never violent. We learn to face the fear of the unpleasant. There is nothing we have to get rid of. We want to treat ourselves with respect and gentleness, not violence. Desires are part of us. It is impossible to stifle them. We can only observe them when we are ready, and find the source of our desire. Mystics tell us to master sexual desire not because sex is wrong but because it is such a great source of power. Mastery doesn't stifle sexual desire. It means we have a choice in how we direct our sexual/creative life energy.

Using conventional language, if someone tells us that we are greedy or grasping, we would probably be very insulted. In spiritual terms, grasping or greed is the natural reaction of the mind when it touches a pleasant sensory object (sight, sound, taste, thought, etc.). Each of these hundreds of impressions produces in us a pleasant, unpleasant, or neutral feeling. These impressions are happening so rapidly that we are not aware of them. For example, we continually change our physical posture to hide the discomfort that is always present.

When we aren't aware of the mind's natural reaction, each time we experience pleasure we want to have more. Grasping or greed doesn't have to do with us personally. It is something that all minds do. Although we can't stop this natural reaction of the mind, we can become aware of it. When the mind knows whether it is experiencing a pleasant, unpleasant, or neutral sensation, it doesn't get stuck. We no longer need to embroider a story around each subtle experience.

Meditation is not to be confused with the cultural ideal of striving for self–improvement. It is not done to relax us, although that is certainly one of the effects, or to make us different than we are. Awareness meditation practice is a means of slowing down and paying close attention to the images, thoughts, and feelings in the mind and the sensations in the body. With practice, we can experience the body as it is: a constant flow of sensory impressions (thinking, seeing, hearing, touching, tasting, smelling). Awareness does not make us uncaring or unable to function in the world. It frees our energy so we can make clear, compassionate choices. The power to direct our life energy without being limited by our fears and grasping is freedom.

SEASONING

Is it enough, our seasoning,
Enough to wisen the way we love?
Seasoning is what makes food taste,
what awakens my palate on a dull day.
Already every neuron fires,
awakening is not the need between us.
Except that as I age I waken further.
You come to startle wide my inner eye,
and place your herbals on my tongue.

Seasoning says the cycles
have already circled round and round.
Nothing wholly new,
the wheel of the year
accustomed to its spiral path.
You feel so familiar
but this moment we share
has never been before,
will never come again.
And the next, and the next, fresh!
This ancient path is virgin.
Yet our seasoning
lays down on the fresh path
a rich layer of lives past.

Seasoning makes wood ready to burn.
in the country
when my woodstove gave the only warmth,
only seasoned wood would do.
Wood that had waited while all its water
bled.
Wood made ready for surrender.
You prepare me and I you, for the fire.
Is it enough, our seasoning?
Shall we grow one day wise enough
to love the way we long to,
to bleed away the fears that keep us green,
to change the vapors of shame,
and burn finally
into something else altogether?

Sue Silvermarie

Some women experience enhanced sexual desire during menopause and after. For me, at least for the moment, the desire has cooled and my responses have changed. I am slower to excite, and my orgasm when it comes is not that great clap of thunder that I used to experience, but a series of summer squalls that follow one another, more intense each time, as if I could go on coming forever. Sandy Boucher

MENOPAUSAL LUST

What I want at 44,
an image I painted in a poem
over twenty years ago:
"She loves as she breathes,
as she eats;
easily, everyday".
Yes, a diet of steady
sexual possibilities.

I know what I am ready for:
regular shedding of separations,
nightly remembering of oneness,
steady sex.
Constant expansion.
Ordinary exploring
of the next
surprise!

Sue Silvermarie

CRYSTAL & SANDY

Crystal

Our relationship began at an artists' retreat in the Southwest and it was a sexually high time for us. The place we were in, both mentally and physically, was sacred. We were away from the city and out in nature everyday and also doing our creative work. I remember one lovemaking experience where although we didn't leave our bodies it felt like we went into another realm. The whole period of time (on retreat) seemed sacred: being in nature, being in the Southwestern culture, and being in a creative space. One day we visited an artist gallery where large, beautiful sculptures of Native American women were on exhibit. Later when we made love it felt like Sandy's face kept changing into the faces we had seen on the sculptures.

Sandy

It was an experience of synchronicity: nature, creative work, sculptures, making love. Several months later we traveled to Asia. During that time I had a deep opening and a strong sense that Crystal had come into my life to open me in that way. It was a conviction I felt during lovemaking. I was having visions and I was also speaking poetry. I was seeing changing scenes and connections were being made for me and then I would speak a haiku. It was an amazing welling up of images. The scenes weren't about my life. The scenes were of people's activities and embedded in the scene would be a pun or verbal concept that illuminated a connection I had not previously realized. The sense was that Crystal had opened me so that I could experience this.

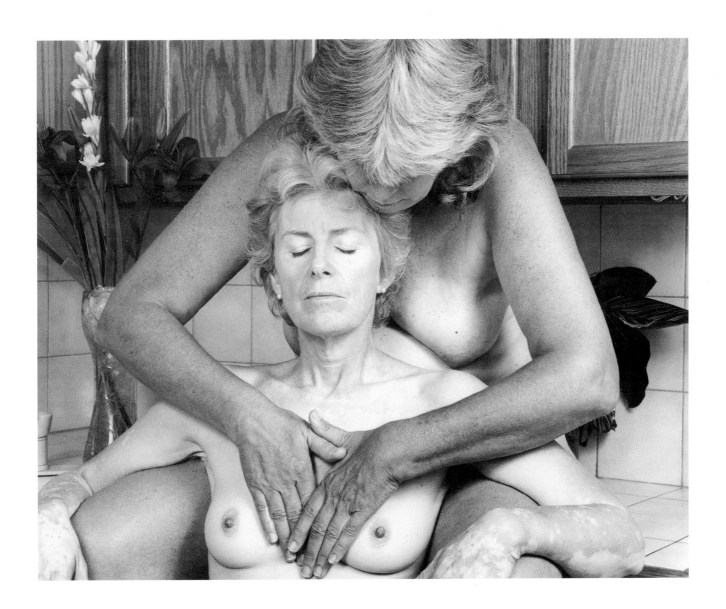

37

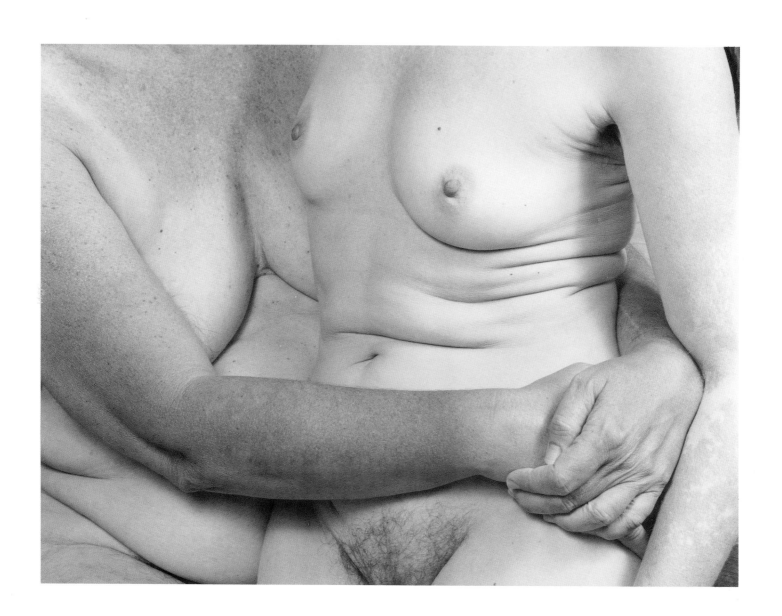

JOY TO THE EARTH

The other day Yeshe (she's my muse, you know) and I were having one of our usual talks about spirituality and sexuality. I was describing my hot flashes. I am talking very hot, so hot that I turn bright red and start to sweat, heavy sweat, dripping from my face and chest. Not only that, there is a definite pause in consciousness. I go someplace else. I never did find out where. I just know I'm not where I was when the hot flash started. Now, that's something that might bear investigation. Do other women go someplace else when they have hot flashes and, if so, do they go to the same place? And, if so, what are all those beautiful, sweaty women doing in that place we don't know the location of? I'd like to mention one other concern. As we sit here talking, the vaginal walls are thinning. So you might not be as moist as you have been accustomed to in the past. And, at those special times when moisture counts the most, you may need a little extra help. So I got myself this little bottle of astro–glide. Astro–glide, guess they thought it would give you a heavenly trip. Well, one day I threw away that astro–glide. No more need for it.

You see, I met another menopausal woman. Both being single, we would often spend weekends together. Now, she didn't have a spare room, she just had a sofa with one of those foldaway beds, but you know how lumpy they can be. So, I chose to sleep with her in her big bed. Well, one night we lay side by side, very still and very proper. The next morning I slipped out of bed very early, just before dawn, as is my usual custom, and went into the bathroom. I felt something sticky on my thighs. I thought, can it be, after all these months, I have my bloods again? Well, I wasn't looking forward to this. I was enjoying their absence, and you can imagine my surprise when I found that sweet, woman cream on my thighs. Could this mean? Well, it was absolutely true. Not only did that magic feeling not leave me, it was filling my whole being and this meant no more astro–glide, thank you.

I told Yeshe that those magic feelings not only don't go away, they get better and stronger. Remember the first night I slept next to my friend? An amazing light show took place inside my body. Shimmering rainbow light rose along my spine, in a continuous stream, rising through my head like a shower of stars. Now I want you to know I have experienced this during meditation, but it never happened to me when lying in bed next to someone. I opened my eyes a bit, like I sometimes do, just to make sure there were no lights in the room, and sure enough the lights were inside me.

I knew it was probably the kundalini rising again. You know, that beautiful serpentine energy that lies coiled at the base of our spines. It's the mother of wisdom, sleeping right there inside us, waiting to wake up and shine like a glorious light through our whole being. What a great gift this is. You may think of it as your first birthday present from the Goddess. Why, it is the Goddess. She's so magnificent that she can give a part of herself to each of us and still be whole and infuse the whole wide world, even the whole universe, with her energy. There we were, lying side by side in the middle of the night and whoosh, the lights went on inside me. I guess I was being a little celestial myself. I didn't even connect this feeling with my friend beside me.

Later, I come to find out that our friends had noticed this magic energy passing between us months earlier when we were all out to dinner. I guess I was the last one to know. Well, I did move fast once it came to my attention. My sweet friend and I planned a special weekend together at her house. In a past life I had been a housewife and mother in New Jersey, so I made use of those skills. Why, not only did I plan all the meals but I cooked them in advance, so all we had to do was heat and serve. Believe me, there was a lot of heat that weekend, if you know what I mean.

So may I talk plainly now? Many women want to know how sex is different in midlife. Well, I can't speak for everyone, but then again, you're not asking me to do that, are you? I can tell you my own experience and see if you have had similar ones. Take orgasms. In my younger days orgasms came quite rapidly. Sometimes I played with the sensations to hold the orgasms back, for a little longer enjoyment. Now it happens naturally–they just come slower and are most enjoyable and, everyone is so different, it's always a surprise. Slower, longer, deeper and richer, more textured. It seems as though lovemaking is wilder because it is more practical, more matter of fact. There is some solidity there that makes the whole experience more grounded and holds it. And in that grounding and holding, there is freedom to fly.

Yes, on that special weekend not only did we fly, but we danced on the Earth and danced on the bottom of the sea. Oh, it was so slow and delicious and then it began to build and build until finally we were off and flying. It is most certainly true about the sustaining power of woman. I know you know that. And it is so clear that this power grows. There is something to be said for taking our sweet time. Now, I know you don't have to be older to do this. What I'm saying now is that you don't have to live in memories. There is a depth that comes from knowing ourselves; it's just plain old life experience, I guess.

Why Yeshe says that we can truly know another person only when we truly know ourselves. And she's the mother of wisdom, so she knows. So picture this, two menopausal women, very wise and knowing of themselves, taking their sweet time to explore and delight each other. Why, that's two women who are getting the best pleasure ever, wouldn't you say that's true?

My sweet friend and I have continued to explore these bodily delights. It is an extravaganza of feelings which my darling often experiences as waves of glorious color sweeping through her body. We have mystical times and earthy times and wild times and sweet times. It is an incredible journey. Oh, there have been times that we have rolled around with the sweat glistening on our bodies pressing us together so tightly we are one glorious being, heaving and sighing. What sounds we make, ooh, those sounds could carry you off into a primeval forest, or deep in the bottom of the sea or off to the highest mountaintop. Yes, dear friend, these are the times that are in store for you or maybe you're already experiencing post–menopausal zest and have a story or two.

Why, there have been times I have melted into my precious lover. That's right, just totally dissolved. Have you had this experience too, just totally dissolved into tiny sparkles of light and then disappeared completely? I tell you, for the next few days, it's hard to walk around. Then there was the time my sweet love turned into the Buddha Tara, right there in my arms. It was an awesome experience that left me speechless, and I'm quite a talker. Another time, at the height of passion, I concentrated all my energy and it made a beam of light that burst off into the stars. What followed was a stillness and a profound sense of the sacred. The energy filled the whole room.

Well, you may be thinking what does all this talk about bodily functions like sex and the menopause have to do with spirituality? I'll tell you, although you may already know, and you probably do. It's very simple. The spirit lives in the body. And spirituality is an exploration of the spirit, a marvelous investigation of the livingness of all things. I feel like we're schoolgirls learning where the spirit dwells and remembering how to act as if all life were sacred. Because it is, you know.

Best of all is making love to your sweetheart from the space of true love. Why, with true love, there is no self. I know, you're thinking, if there is no self, then who is making love? Just let me say this. Once we realize we have no self, it doesn't mean we stop existing. It means we're not self–centered, and you know how tiring that is when somebody is self–centered. Why, they can be most unpleasant to be around. Or a body can be too centered on the other person. I know you know how tiring that is. Why, you try to rescue everybody and you don't have clear boundaries. Oh, it goes on and on. So, what we truly want is to be centered on all things. That way we don't cling. No more saran wrap relationships. Why, being just plain centered is so special, it's the cure for worry. When we can move through life without clinging, we aren't worried or anxious, we don't get upset or confused. It's a good life. We're free and that makes for joy, honey, yes, absolute delight.

There was the time my sweet friend and I were entwined in a meadow full of irises, on top of a hill, overlooking the ocean on a bright sunny day. Why, it was two goddesses delighting in each other. Now, I think that's the way to bring joy to the Earth, don't you?

letters to kate

*we sit in the kitchen the older one and i two women of laughter and salt. the
back door swings wide you are here lights dance round yr head i am here you
say we move together fingers test body's solidity eyes scan for the shore and
i am virgin again in this house of dusk and magic. at the baths we wash each
other of silence of the sharp pain of not being whole. the tide surges in it
roars in our ears i sway to keep my balance and all the while these small
tender moments curled in the corners these gestures of love and sorrow. you
are here not somewhere else i am here and what does it mean.*

*that when the pomegranate finally falls it is ripe and filled with juice. yr
thighs are milky white streaked with sweet red blood they are koi slipping
through my fingers. the water's surface is far above. you are the water i rain
on you i rain fire you flame up to meet me yr scales incandescent open open
we are bow and arrow night sky trajectory obsidian mirror into past into
future those we have been crowd the room they laugh and dance until we
explode into sleep.*

Joan Iten Sutherland

LOVE IN AGE

All bliss known on earth I have found
In you, Woman, Lover–Beloved;
Beyond reason loved; beyond care
Of self or safety in the passionate years
When youth must find—cost no matter—
Haven or Heaven.
                    And now
                        in age
Your Being mirrors the Divinity.

You have taken me beyond transport
To nether worlds where no man,
Though brave, travels willing (but, quaking,
To regain wife or life)
                    shown me
The fury figure of Kali death–dancing on
My ravished hopes;
                    yet, from them,
from their silt and muck
                    reborn
What nourishes the soul.

Woman, so gentle in my arms
Loving, you have opened to me
Fierce, my own dark heart
And found therein and to me reflected
My source of light.

Here on this bed holding you
In passion–shattered wonder, lip to lip
Limb twined with limb
In oblivion of Thee and Me,
Breathing our mingled sweat,
Juices spilled out
                    mutually anointing

Here on this bed, holding you
So human in your need
                        (and knowing mine)
Miraculous, the human veil is rent.

Lover–beloved, Woman
Small and strong in my arms
                    I know in you
The Goddess
            Mystery
                fecund Emptiness
From which all fullness comes
And universes flower.

Elsa Gidlow, 1974

PELE'S BREATH, A LESBIAN FIRE MEDITATION

The Goddess Pele lives in Hawaiian hearts and minds as the supreme personification of volcanic majesty and power, in a universe in which all natural forces are regarded as life forces, and related to human life.

Sit comfortably, with your spine erect, if possible. Take a few deep breaths. Let your thoughts settle. Imagine yourself standing at the edge of a small rainforest: The huge trees and ferns are glistening with raindrops. Stand quietly and ask Pele if you may enter the forest. Receive her welcome. Begin slow, steady walking downhill through the forest until you reach the blackened bed of lava. Gather a few small stones to make an altar on the blackened earth and continue your walk across Pele's belly. See before you the place where her breath, in streams of steam, rises from the earth. Lie down and let her breath warm and soothe your body, your bones, your heart. Breathe deeply and let Pele fiercely and tenderly nourish your lesbian body, your lesbian mind, your lesbian heart. Accept Pele's acknowledgement and blessing of your integrity, your being, your opening truth into the world.

Breathe in the breath of Pele, feel her fire, her energy caress your feet, move up through your legs and heat your yoni. Keep breathing as the breath of Pele fills your yoni, your belly and spirals upward through your spine. Sense Pele's energy filling your heart. Imagine the energy, the warm breath circling from your heart back into your belly and rising up again into your heart. Heart to belly, belly to heart, Pele's fire warms you, fills you.

Sense Pele's fire in your heart. Feel the energy rising into your throat and circling back into your heart. Heart to throat. Throat to heart, the fire of Pele illuminates you. Come again to your throat: Sense the warm opening there as Pele's breath touches you. Sense the energy spiraling up through your third eye* and into the crown of your head. Imagine the swirling breath touch your crown and spiral down to your throat. Throat to crown, crown to throat, the energy circles around.

Breathe deeply, easily, allowing Pele's warm breath to nourish and energize you. Sense the energy at the top of your head, above your head, and sense it spiraling down, above the head and into the heart. Energy dancing from heart and up above your head. Head to heart and from the heart down into belly. Heart to belly, belly to heart. Sense the energy move from your heart to your feet and from your feet up through your heart to above your head. You are Pele's daughter. She has breathed life into you: fire, light, life, inspiration, creative power. Fire, power, breath of Pele. Breathe together. You are of the Earth. You are of the fire. You are of the air. You are of the water. You are Pele's daughter, sister, lover, friend. You are that open. Trust it.

Now continue to breathe slowly and deeply and gently let the images dissolve. Take a few minutes to sit quietly in the stillness. Then gently rock your body from side to side and when you feel ready, stand up.

*The third eye is located in the middle of the forehead. It is an energy center or chakra.

JOURNAL ENTRY, December 29

Barbara and I are going through a rocky period. Dealing with the daily pain from arthritis in my spine and joints, as well as the debilitating symptoms I experience from multiple chemical sensitivities, is challenging for us both. It feels like there are three entities in our relationship: the two of us and the illness. We need a safe place in which to reconnect.

I found a marvelous picture of Pele, her hair waves of fire extending out from her head. She stood, a fiery being in the ocean, and curled within her heart was the body of a woman. I placed it on our altar and Barbara and I sat together and repeated our vows. I was amazed at how instantly I centered. I felt my energy relax and extend down into the earth and reach out into the stars. I felt secure. We breathed together and envisioned an infinity symbol, each within her own space, each connected to the other. I asked that we call upon Pele, thank her for cradling us to her breast, for exposing any pain or confusion. I asked for direction: What will grow here? What path will we take?

INTIMATE RELATIONSHIPS

We strive to find relationships that are mutually satisfying. We ask ourselves, Am I getting enough of my needs met to stay involved in an intimate relationship with my partner? We work to be able to speak our needs, to communicate clearly, to negotiate. We want pleasant and/or exciting companions, trust, loyalty, and passion. Without negating these needs can we open out into a wider perspective of relationship? Can we look in a practical way at our relationships and ask if the relationship serves life? Do we add to the clarity or the confusion? Do we build or do we destroy? Do we create peace or conflict? Do we hurt or do we heal?

Each time the heart opens, the power of love is strengthened. In this way, strong relationships are gifts to the world. A strong relationship is an inter–relationship: not one in which we depend on the other to express what we can't but one in which each partner is committed to helping the other achieve the fullest expression of herself. The more openness there is in love, the more energy there is to share and give to the world.

A lesbian woman is drawn to a union and merger with another woman, to a kind of participation mystique, *which involves a deep identity with the loved one. This union, which is a numinous experience, beyond the personal, also deeply embodies the personal.* Karin Loftus Carrington

THE OPENING OF THE HEART

In that moment I knew what I held in my hands was not of
　　　　shell and ocean but of flesh and bone
I had enfolded her within my own wetness
　　　　and in the sweetness of her yielding
I found her heart
　　　　a golden glow of tears and sorrow yet to be touched
I whispered into the hinge of her clam
　　　　so tightly closed that not even water could enter
I whispered over and over into the bitterness of her unyielding
I said I would never cease whispering until her fear released her
I said I would continue to whisper even when I was gone

The opening of the heart is not a joy but a deep pain
　　　　that cracks open every seam and stitch
　　　　until the fabric itself is gone
I whispered over and over into the sweetness of her yielding

The opening of the heart is not a pain but a deep joy
　　　　that flows out when every seam and stitch cracks open
　　　　that unravels thread by thread
　　　　until even the fabric itself is gone
I whispered over and over to the sweetness of her healing

The opening of your heart never ceases
It comes in on the tide
　　　　of breath
It goes out on the tide
　　　　of breath
The whisperings of a lover
　　　　a chant, a song, a prayer
　　　　to your wholeness
　　　　to the sacred awakening of the heart

Marcelina Martin, 1990

HALLIE & GWEN

Hallie

All sexuality is sacred to me because each person is holy. I go into a very sacred place when I am making love. When my partner Gwen and I were first coming together the only way I could describe our connection was to say that it seemed prehuman. It seemed to originate in a time before either of us—or even any person—was human. This was a very unusual experience for me, as though we originally were part of the same fragment of star that had exploded and we were reuniting. I don't even think in terms of past lives or soul mates so I was very struck by that experience.

I've noticed that when I'm making love after having been out in a particularly beautiful place in nature that I instantly feel that my body and/or my lover's body are that part of the Earth where we have been. For instance, we recently spent a short time overlooking the Waipi'o Valley in Hawaii—a beautiful green chasm that is a thousand feet deep and almost a half-mile across, an incredible place. Later on that night when we were making love I suddenly felt that my body was the Waipi'o Valley, vast and deep and green. I think what happens is that I remember that my body is the Earth's body, particularly when I'm making love.

The other night I was lying in bed with Gwen and suddenly I saw her body as being all purple and yellow, the colors of the flowers I had picked that day. I'm reminded constantly that we are part of the Earth, there is no real separation between us. Sacred sexuality brings that understanding forth.

MIMA & KIM

Mima

Making love to Kim is like making a prayer. She focuses her honest feeling on me...I hear the sounds of the ocean. I hear the waves. I feel a freedom and a space opening up as boundaries melt away and I become one with everything.

Kim

Like music, there is a precision and rhythm in love making. There are eyes at the ends of my fingertips. Everything comes alive, and I feel the pulse of life running through me.

LONGING FOR UNION

In lesbian relationships there is the strong desire to merge and reclaim lost parts of ourselves. This desire to merge, the heart's longing for union/reunion, holds the possibility for a powerful transformation. Our capacity to feel empathy and compassion is a primary reason we find lesbians in the forefront of civil rights, animal rights, deep ecology, and all organizations and movements for equality and rights for women, children and oppressed peoples.

In her essay "Women Loving Women," from the book *Same–Sex Love*, Karin Lofthus Carrington describes archetypal patterns of lesbian love. In the pattern most relevant for our exploration of sacred sexuality, the women reunite not only with each other and the wholeness within themselves, but with the world. Carrington borrows Joanna Macy's metaphoric "world as lover, world as self" to describe the pattern in which a woman remembers her wholeness through a reunion with the lover/mother. In this pattern each woman is both mother and daughter, and the mother with whom they are reunited is life itself.

This archetypal pattern of reunion/union with the Mother Earth is clearly expressed in Native American cosmology. Prayers, rituals, and healing modalities all confirm the knowledge that we are not separate from the Earth or from each other, but that we are all interconnected in the web of life. Because of these deep connections we can awaken to the knowledge of our wholeness and our responsibility to the whole.

Sexuality and spirituality are facilitated by a deep intimacy with one's inner nature, with the physical body, and intimacy with the natural world. This intimacy brings a quality of loving connection and sensitivity to life. It is energetic, spontaneous, and joyful. Sexual or creative energy radiates through all life. Erotic, creative, divine, Goddess energy. Fertile, rich, passionate, abundant energy. There is nothing—that is, no–thing—that exists outside of or is untouched by this energy. It is life itself and as such is sacred. The sexual act is but one expression of this energy. We make our sex sacred, in the same way we make any life experience sacred, through our intention.

What makes sex or any other activity in my life sacred is a sense of letting go, surrendering myself to a supreme openness and receptivity which requires trust in myself, my partner and in the grace of the experience. Patti

THE SHADOW IN INTIMATE RELATIONSHIPS

S exual love can open us to new perceptions of reality and allows us to touch the deepest source of life. I have found that it requires an openness, a sensitivity, and a willingness to take risks. For myself, openness is not possible without surrender, a release of fears and tightly held perceptions about myself and the world. An intimate sexual relationship with a woman provides both the safety and the joy in similarity. Women know how a woman's body feels, how a woman's mind thinks, how a woman's emotions flow. In the arms of our beloved, we find a mirror, a reflection of ourselves. The mirror is an incredibly powerful image. A mirror does not judge; it only reflects. The mirror has no attitude, prejudice, or belief about what it sees; it simply reflects. The gift and the power of a lesbian relationship is the strength of that mirror. We have another being like ourselves giving us the reflection. This essential sameness, the familiarity we experience with other women, can be a powerful means for us to recognize our own strength and beauty.

This mirror also gives us the opportunity to see the shadow, the aspects of self we have kept hidden in the dark. When the shadowy parts of our personalities unconsciously interact, the dynamic can be negative and often destructive. Working with the shadow is uncomfortable, yet, if we are willing to face the fear and allow the shadow to surface, it can be shared on a conscious level. This sharing provides a rich and fertile space for growth and transformation. We directly experience our intrinsic wholeness. We come to know we are holy.

Transformational processes are not without danger. In the union and reunion we experience in lesbian relationships, the ego boundaries are dissolved. When this experience of dissolving is fully integrated, we come in touch with great reservoirs of compassion and kindness. We sense the reality that is beyond the personal ego, the physical self, and we awaken to the inter-relationship of all life. When it is not integrated, we become swallowed up, enmeshed in each other's shadow, and we lose our grounding and sense of personal integrity.

The shadow is a Jungian* concept I have found useful in my growing self-awareness. In dreams, the shadow is the personification of certain aspects of the unconscious. However, Jung cautioned against thinking of the shadow in a limiting way and said that the shadow could describe the whole of the unconscious. The shadow can be problematic in Western culture where

*Carl Jung was a Swiss psychologist and scholar in comparative religion. His views contrasted sharply with the prevailing Freudian psychology, especially with regards to its attitudes towards sexuality and the sacred.

we have a strong split between what we consider negative and positive, good and bad, right and wrong. In every human being there exists an intuitive drive towards wholeness. We both hope for and fear connection with the source of life. When we don't address the complete picture and continue to split into polarities, we are open to many harmful distortions, including the lack of clear boundaries, the danger of enmeshment, and a wide range of fearful, aggressive, and prejudicial attitudes and behaviors. All of us contain within us both generosity and greed, kindness and hatred, wisdom and ignorance. To fully develop our generosity, kindness, and wisdom, we must be willing to see and work with our greed, hatred, and ignorance. We cannot realize our wholeness until we embrace our shadow.

Here is an example of the shadow. Suppose I fear that I won't get my needs for intimacy met, that my lover won't be there for me in an emotional way. Maybe this happened in past relationships or maybe my parents weren't there for me. So I keep projecting this fear outward by focusing too much on my partner. I work too hard on the relationship. I create a whole lot of conversation and emotionality. I might try to anticipate all my lover's needs. I stare at her often and force intimacy inappropriately. My behavior becomes exaggerated and artificial because it is coming out of the shadow, from fear.

The shadow problem becomes even stickier when the shadows of both couples interact. Suppose my partner felt invaded by her parents or past lovers. She fears that she won't have enough space. Her unconscious fear is expressed by overcontrolling. She might want to make most of the decisions in the relationship. She may have a hard time sharing finances. She may have rigid attitudes about everything from politics to how to clean the house. She will try to protect herself by keeping emotional distance.

We may end up fighting, withdrawing, or resisting because our worst fears are realized. One of us has no space and the other has no closeness. If we are willing to work together we can begin to negotiate difficult places. My partner might need to say "I need twenty minutes to decompress when I get home from work." We agree not to engage until she has this time. I might need to ask specifically for what I want. For example, "Could I have ten minutes to talk about something that is upsetting me?" When our fears come to light the circumstances between us become less charged. While there probably won't be radical personality changes there will be a lessening of expectations and more ability to see what is happening in the moment without distorting the situation with heavy baggage from the past.

BELONGING LIGHTS OUR WAY

You say you belong to me.
I become frightened.
Then I remember the stars
belonging to each other.
I think how the wind
belongs to the sky.
This is the way I belong to you.
We hitch our rides
without controlling when or how.
What makes me fear belonging when
belonging lights our way to one another.
Sweet self of my Self,
my molecules respond to you by rearranging.
Recognition reshapes me.
We are self seeking self,
and the seeking has gone liveslong.
I want to know your body.
What we have to teach each other
comes through our bodies.
I belong to you the way
I belong to the Mother,
I rest in you.
You belong to me the way
you belong to the stars.
In my arms you dream deeply.
My fears dissolve,
we meet as equals in a new time
a time of no shame.

What we have to teach each other
spreads from the heart,
the way my pleasure
spreads from between my legs.
I lay the gift of finding you
on the altar, giving it back,
turning over to the Mother all fears.
Laughing in joy
to Her I lift up
this gift

Sue Silvermarie

HYMN TO A MYSTERY

Your Woman Flower blooms
To my touch
        opens
To probing kiss; I, bee
To its honey, plunge
To being's core.

Warm, convolute,
What marvel of function;
Sepal, petal: part
Them, find stamen,
Stigma stiff to finger,
The cryptic ovary
Secreting nectar.
Phoenix flesh that
Living, dies
To live again
In ecstasy.

Warm Woman Flower,
Apotheosis
Of all life's cooler blooms,
On what altar, with
What mass shall I
Celebrate
Your mystery?

Elsa Gidlow, 1967

WOLF & ANTONIA

Antonia

In my relationship with Wolf I felt there was an awakening of my whole being, parts of myself that I didn't even know existed. Every persona that showed its face met a sparring partner in Wolf. I'd had plenty of sex before Wolf and it was always wonderful. But there was a part of me that was removed, a private part confined to myself. It seemed like I was watching or making a commentary about it.

Wolf was someone who blew the doors open. There was a total focus on my being, not my mind or thoughts, or the place I was in. It was a presence of being that had nothing to do with time or space. Some times in lovemaking I would be completely blown away and have to stop and take a deep breath because I couldn't feel where my body stopped and hers began. There would be a oneness, yet my sense of self was very much intact. The physical became a vehicle we used to get to a place outside of time and space. Two spirits coming together. It felt like two flames being magnetized towards each other in a void of blackness. Two fires burning brightly and suddenly I was in a huge blaze. Each fire still has its core but the flames were licking wildly, creating something more than just two flames. The sensation of my belly touching her belly would be the trigger. That was the spark, everything stemmed from there. It still is to this day. We can touch every other part of our bodies, we can have sex and yet there is something special about the two bellies coming together. It's like plugging into an outlet.

That kind of intensity hasn't been there consistently throughout our seven–year relationship. At times we get tired, caught up in daily routines or focused on a goal like school or traveling. When the intensity isn't present there is a deep sadness and yearning for it. However, I have come to trust that we are deeply connected and that with all of life's many demands and distractions there will always be many reunions and heated explorations—it just takes that one spark.

64

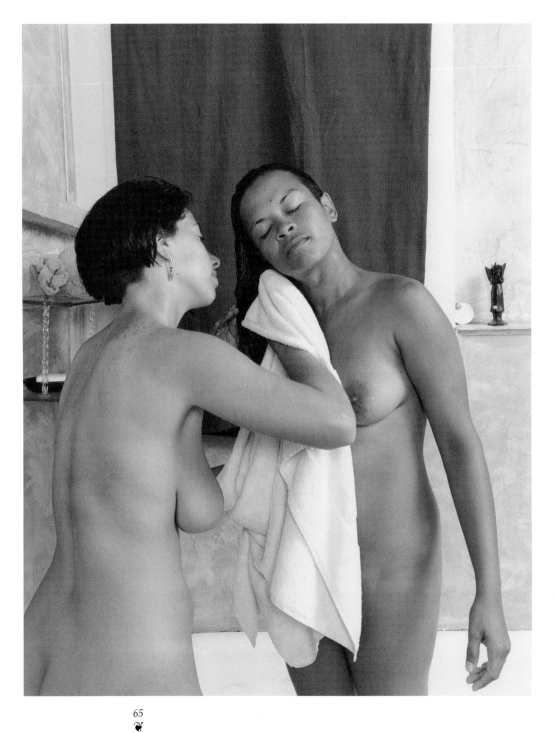

Wolf

All my life is spiritual and sacred. There is a sacredness that is more than simply sexual desire, it is the desire that creates life. In sex with Antonia the desire becomes so pure. I want something. I feel like there are the two of us and then a third entity is created out of pure desire.

When I am in the heat of passion making love with Antonia there is an energy of the past, ancestral energy, surrounding us. At this point there is a doorway that opens up and allows me contact with the animal desire that is inside me. It is a natural desire, an instinct, that is opened and the energy pours in. The intellectual garbage goes away. The compartmentalized intellectual mind goes and I am there with the sensory self. All of the sensory elements are noticed, the sounds, the smells, and Antonia and I are in this interior realm, getting more in touch with our animal selves.

The times when the energy has been stronger have a lot to do with breathing. There is no time when we know it is going to happen. We are breathing in sync and there is an urge that I don't hold back. It is a letting go of the surfaces of the skin, where the skin meets and there is a lessening of containment. It is an energy field. It moves from the sensory into an energy field. Nothing matters except that one orgasmic moment. At times the orgasm isn't even needed. It is a feeling, not a physical orgasm, an internal energy orgasm.

With my totem being the wolf there is a great amount of respect and homage I place within that form. When the sexual energy is at full force, with that animal sensory energy to the forefront, it is like looking through strange eyes, eyes other than my own. There is a dance, it is hard to explain in words. I understand the feeling but the words become trite. It is like a journey, not a long stretched-out journey, but an instantaneous journey where I move from my body and my eyes and I go through a doorway and move into a pure sensory place which expands into a burst of energy. The dance doesn't happen in a physical, tangible way. There is a recognition. I recognize who Antonia is. I recognize my own animal sense clearly. There isn't a physical form. It is beyond that, just swirling energy.

Only a few times this happened with us. We would be engaged in sex and at the high point of our exchange with each other there would be an image, almost like an illusory animal form. Holographic imagery flying out at me in animal form. If the energy is coming towards me I see the visual form and Antonia feels it. And it also happens the other way around. I feel an image lunging from me and Antonia sees it. We would both react. We would stop, saying, did you see that? Did you see that? It hasn't happened often, maybe three times. By the third time we learned to accept it rather than stop. It was a little scary when we first began our relationship. Maybe not scary, just unusual. Now it is a little more familiar and it happens less.

Marcelina photographed us in our bedroom where our altar takes up about a fifth of the space. Our bed is placed directly in front of the altar. We can't help but be aware that this is a place where we also pray. Often if the candles are going or we have just prayed before we get into bed, and begin to become sexual, some of that energy carries into our lovemaking. We didn't pray with that intention but because we are in a sacred place it has an effect.

Sometimes our breathing comes into sync. We have talked about doing it consciously but have not tried it yet. When our breathing does come into sync it is so outrageous. We don't add anything extra, there is no music playing. It is just one body turned on to another body and that is very spiritual. It is a quiet experience, a deep, internal activity in the bedroom. It is not the same in other rooms in our house.

We go camping a lot and make love outdoors. There is a different sensation outdoors and I believe it is being so much more aware of the environment, the ground, the trees. I'm more aware of my physical grounding and my physical body. It is always wild, hot sex and at the same time it doesn't go as far deep in as when we make love in our bedroom with the altar. It's all wonderful and enjoyable and outdoors sex is more playful but it is on a lighter level. I feel very connected to the earth and the trees, and the deep connection to nature somehow makes the sex not as deep in the energy process. I take in more of nature on a tangible level. It doesn't go as deep on an intangible level. Nature intensifies the physicality, the rawness, the potency of sex. Physical passion is more outdoors and the depth of the internal passion is more indoors.

One Sound

The sound, the human sound.
I cry out when we join in love,
I cry out against our separation.
You tell me to cry out for myself.

You lie in the water thighs spread open
while I wash you
circling in slow motion with sandalwood soap
your parts no longer marked as private.
Simply flower, centerplace.
We reverse the blessing.
I find no shred of shame remains.

Before bed you bless me again
wrapping me on the table with the silk blanket.
I have waited since I was torn from my mother
for the healing you lay upon me with your palms.

For the words
heard by the cells of my body.
Your touch at the base of my spine
brims my pelvic bowl;
a shimmer of Love.

I wake in the final night beside you
with a dream of jumping,
horses jumping over obstacles.
Myself the flying flesh
meeting joy and challenge.
You wake at the same time
dredge from your dream the word, bright!
Then you bring up butterflies.
I follow with you their seamless motion.

Now the great bird has lifted you away again.
This time I stay to watch at the window
hand against the glass
until the speck of your plane is beyond my seeing.

Our spinning begins.
In the cocoon our love will change.
When we welcome it next,
we greet a new shape.
Walking away, dazed,
inside me sounds a cry.
One sound,
our love, our death.

Sue Silvermarie

LOVE'S ENERGY

The purpose of this exercise is a loving, sensuous exchange of energy. It is not necessary to do the exercise in a seated position. Nor is it necessary to physically gaze into each other's eyes. Please feel free to adapt this exercise to physical abilities and desires. For example the lovers could be lying side by side mentally envisioning the energy exchange.

Sit naked, back to back. Take time to ground yourself by breathing deeply. You may want to imagine the base of your spine like a giant root extending deep into the heart of the Earth. Imagine breathing energy from the earth up along your spine. When you feel grounded, allow that image to dissolve and without losing your grounding become sensitive to the sensation of your back touching your lover's back.

Lover one imagines breathing the energy drawn from the base of her lover's spine up along her own spine and exhales the energy out the top of her crown chakra. She continues breathing in this manner.

Lover two imagines receiving her partner's energy through her crown chakra like a waterfall, and allows the energy to descend down her spine. She exhales the energy through the base of her spine. She continues breathing in this manner.

The lovers continue to sit back to back breathing the energy from one to the other and feeling the circle of energy. Now the lovers may want to imagine sending colors through their spines. Continue to breathe colors and be aware of the sensations and feelings that arise during this exercise.

Without losing the sense of this circle of energy, the lovers slowly turn to face one another. With eyes open and soft, continue to sense one another's energy. It is not necessary to try to maintain the visualization. Simply be aware of your breath and keep your eyes focused on your lover's eyes. Be open to any feelings, emotional or sexual, that arise. Keep softening and opening to the gaze of your lover. Allow yourself to see and to be seen. Be sensitive to any energy changes. You may want to increase contact with touching, kissing, and lovemaking. Move slowly and keep eye contact as much as possible. You may choose to complete the exercise without increased contact. Slowly move apart from each other, while maintaining eye contact. Take a deep breath, close your eyes, and imagine your roots deep into the Earth. When you are ready, open your eyes.

LOVEMAKING AS WORSHIP

I have had experiences in lovemaking where I lose all sense of a personal self, myself or my lover. My lover becomes a Goddess or the Buddha Tara, and I am her devotee. My love for her reaches out to the world. It is the ultimate act of surrender, of opening into the universe. I come naked with the dearest thing I have to offer, my body, my self, and I offer it to my beloved. In our union we are united not with ourselves alone but with the body of the universe. Lovemaking becomes an act of worship.

Sometimes I play with my breath during lovemaking. I keep my breath slow and steady, resisting my body's urge to quicken. The slow, steady, deep breathing coupled with intense and pleasurable sensations creates a tremendous expansion. I become open to vast reservoirs of energy within myself and my lover. The transformation of energy is tangible. I open out into the universe and there is no gap or separation between me and the universe. It is one seamless, shimmering net of life. It is sacred space.

JOURNAL ENTRY, March 22

Suggestion for a woman whose sexual needs are much less than her partner's. Make your sexual loving an act of devotion. Your partner is the Goddess and you are performing a selfless act of devotion, surrendering totally to the Goddess. You offer her the best you have, that is yourself, your body, your heart. Bring this attitude to your sexual loving. It is pure surrender.

Suggestion for a woman whose sexual needs are much greater than her partner's. Practice gratitude. Fully receive and appreciate the sexual love and attention you do receive. Explore your feelings. Notice the feelings/thoughts you have that it isn't enough, it isn't how you want it to be. Breathe and mentally bow to these thoughts. Now imagine filling your body and mind with a feeling of gratitude. Mentally say: I am joyful and thankful for these moments of sexual love.

Suggestions for both partners. Create a small love altar with yoni symbols and pictures or statues of the Goddess of Love. Make this altar beautiful and sensual. Choose beautiful, vibrant colors and textures. Make a time each day to sit and breathe together in front of the altar.

DOUBLE PHOENIX

She speaks burgundy birds
blue gold wings   flowers indolent on her breasts
she moves slowly her hair curled tightly
hands skimming my thighs she whispers   into my ear
I want you   *my vulva shivers clenches*
her mouth takes me her
tongue tells long dancing stories of flight stars darkness burst
fingers flicker in my bones
she enters me in the moment when my blood begs her
hard deep light lifts from my lips
whirls   moves tightly her mouth shivers
birds appear in my hands
my toes skim stars
I'm wings in the night sky crying out in her breasts
my hips wet flowers

Chrystos

LOVE AND SPONTANEITY

Love and sexual communion take on a spiritual and mystical character when they are spontaneous. Spontaneity doesn't mean that sexual encounters or intimate time cannot be planned. It means that the time itself is unhurried and there are no expectations of what will occur.

There were green plantains, which we half–peeled and then planted, fruit–deep, in each other's bodies until the petals of skin lay like tendrils of broad green fire upon the curly darkness between our upspread thighs. There were ripe red finger bananas, stubby and sweet, with which I parted your lips gently, to insert the peeled fruit into your grape–purple flower.

I held you, lay between your brown legs, slowly playing my tongue through your familiar forests, slowly licking and swallowing as the deep undulations and tidal motions of your strong body slowly mashed ripe banana into a beige cream that mixed with the juices of your electric flesh. Our bodies met again, each surface touched with each other's flame, from the tips of our curled toes to our tongues, and locked into our own wild rhythms, we rode each other across the thundering space, dripped like light from the peak of each other's tongue. Audre Lorde

SHE/I

By the side of the rippling river
we curled together in a cranny
all October afternoon.
She/I, I/She.
Every now and then when
we lifted eyes to look,
long grass waved high above our faces

By the side of the running river,
She/I, I/She,
without fighting the memories,
flowed into lives from before.
Into bodies that
stretched and became and changed and went on.
Loving. Pushing. Begging entrance.

Curved fingers curled into wet caverns,
curved bodies
curled through one another into the earth.
We met and joined, rested,
rested into one another.
With our fingers we listened
to the tumbling dance.

By the side of the rushing river
we kissed and kissed
and kissed so deep,
we fell away from time.
When the sun sank low and we rose,
She/I, I/She
no longer recognized ourselves.

To watch over our ecstasy
the willow behind us
had deferred her dying.
Broken open, she wept in the wind for our joy.
Tender blessings the gentle guardian
had waited to bestow.
She/I, I/She. Broken open.

Sue Silvermarie

NANCY & BONNIE

I was 32 when I tested positive and I made the decision never to have sex or intimacy again. I had just broken up with my girlfriend and my life was a mess. My health was good then. I think my decision was premature. I was frightened about the possibilities. I gave up on living. I had a really strong feeling that I was poison. I used to say in a joking way that I was a poisoned person. I didn't have sex with anyone for four years. I was into the death part of HIV. I thought I was a dead person, just waiting to die. It was very sacred for me to learn that I wasn't a poison person. I couldn't have learned that without sex. Before I was embracing death, I had given up. I had given up on any kind of intimacy with anyone. I was so alone.

I was 36 when I met Bonnie and I was totally smitten. My relationship with her changed my attitude about who I am and particularly who I am with this disease. On a day-to-day level I've realized that I'm not just a person waiting to die. I can live my life. It has been very life–affirming. Now, I don't feel so frightened, I'm more comfortable. I don't even think I was afraid of giving the disease to someone else. I felt that if I approached someone they would react in such a way that I would feel totally rejected. I didn't want to take that chance. I've had a hard time with this disease in the lesbian community. I haven't always been received graciously. It's nice to meet people who can see beyond my HIV status.

When we first started having sex I was self–conscious. At first I was rigid, no you can't do this to me, you can't do that to me. And they were all things I really loved. I wanted to have that flowing sex with someone who didn't have any boundaries. Bonnie really broke down a lot of my rigidity. We have changed a lot about what we think is safe sex and what isn't. In the passion of our new relationship we did a lot of things that we don't do now. Truthfully, I don't love safe sex. I would like sex to be more spontaneous, without any planning, but it can't always be that way. This is the 1990's and there is this new disease and a lot of old diseases too. I think lesbians tend to be cavalier about AIDS—we don't think we can get it.

Sacredness, when I was younger, meant the grass, the trees, the lakes. Now that I am in my late thirties I think what is really sacred is to be able to be comfortable in a hostile world, to feel like there is something that makes you able to live in the day–to–day world. Something that gives you a cushion. That is what is sacred.

79
❧

Close Your Eyes

Come

into a deep dark flower   night woman   inside

crescent moon petals   Scratch your back on this magenta

Roll around in scarlet   Wake Up   Open fur lips

eat your saffron supper   Like her   Tongues in your fingers

taste her midnight bloom with thirsty skin

Hold her petals of teal   lime   russet   silver

white light gold grass on a summer sleeping hill

stroke this blue gray cradle   These petal colors of dreamtime

realtime in her hidden flower   Here!   Listen!   Now melts

Take off your think about it clothes

Leave your answers in the closet

Come for her petals glowing   eyes open along your arms

in this place   her secret mouth   her planting smell   We'll wet

these snow petals   pale peach petals

early morning lavender petals

See her in the deep holding time   floating colortime

coming hometime   Climb into her silver melon breast

held in the noplace of petals   Downy

Here's a dance singing

here's a place to gurgle   laugh   sucking

warm sweet   sweet in her curly midnight flower

Lotus of a thousand skies   Each color an opening

your eyes lick her

sun yellow   moon blue   pine green   sunrise pink

into her night flower   her moon bloom

inside her dark fur corolla

Roll yourself wet

red   salmon   sepia   mud brown   violet   gold

Paint your mouth in petals

Stay

Chrystos

JOURNAL ENTRY, April 26

Sunday morning we made love and I spontaneously began to practice keeping my breathing slow, deep, and even, throughout the lovemaking. I was able to sustain the energy of my orgasms past the point where the sensations are usually so intense that I become tired and have to stop. I was able to enjoy the enormously pleasurable sensations without losing consciousness or being overwhelmed by them. I felt as though I kept opening and opening and opening. The space was vast. I was definitely in my body and enjoying my body, and at the same time conscious of a vast reality beyond any physical constructs. The words *body of the universe* came into my mind. They repeated continuously as if a silent mantra. Perhaps this mantra was symbolic of the intensity of the connection to all living I was experiencing in that moment. The words *body of the universe* seemed to hum in my ear. There was no sense of distraction. I maintained contact with my lover and opened into a vast consciousness that was not separate from my body. My body and the body of my lover became the body of the universe. My individual self dissolved into this joy.

This is the fundamental tantric realization, that the world is pervaded by a Divine Goodness or Goddess. This realization overcomes the mundane dualistic state of thinking. I knew in my whole body the underlying unity of the phenomenal world.

SINCE SAPPHO

Since Sappho
Lesbian poets have written
Of the sweet ache
A womon feels in her breasts
When she loves
A womon
And I don't know
What new there is to say:
How the ocean
That flows blood in our veins
Resonates
To the moon of desire
That lives in us
How the sameness
All the comfort shared
In being female
Does not negate the sizzle
Of polarity
The yin and yang
Of younger, older,
Lighter, darker
Softer, harder,
Paired opposites without
Opposition
But all these things
Have been said before
Since Sappho
Took the muse unto herself
Lesbian poets
Have made love with our words
And have rolled on our tongues
Like quicksilver
This pulsing siren's song.

Barbara Ruth

LOVEMAKING AND THE PSYCHIC DOMAIN

In *Another Mother Tongue*, Judy Grahn describes different domains or levels of power in lesbian lovemaking. Here she describes "the psychic domain" which is beyond the physical and mental domain:

...the beloved does not attempt to control what the lover is doing. She gives her body to the lover. Nor does the lover try to force something to happen.... The lover lets her own spontaneous sensibilities, as she tunes herself to the beloved, tell her what to do, her fingers and her tongue, eyes and ears, and all her body and mind, and she will find she can "see" what to do with her fingers and tongue and become so sensitive as to experience a kind of orgasm—just from stroking the beloved's neck or head or breasts or cervix—through her fingers, the firesticks.

...The experience is that of taking a journey to sources of power and creativity, of "making" something, and of being made. Of going somewhere and coming back different. Intimacy and pleasure and intense feelings, though present, are not the goals; orgasm is present but is not the goal. In fact, the construction of goals destroys the state of feeling, turns it aside, lowers it into the realm of fantasy and the necessity for control. When the creative sexual state proceeds on its own, the feeling or experience is prolonged, ecstatic, emotional, journeylike and with intensity barely short of orgasm over a long period of time; and though the orgasm when it finally and brilliantly happens may culminate in an image or sequence of images, its purpose seems more to be to bring the dreamer back, to return the beloved to the material plane. She is not only coming, she is coming back into herself. *And she has been away, in the sexual/psychic domain. The orgasm is the way back from the trance.*

Grahn tells us these experiences do not need any physical discipline:

...they do require emotional discipline. This includes openness, trust, honesty, and a willingness to display both vulnerability and strength with each other. This means each person needs to have a well-developed femme side and a well-developed butch side.

Lovemaking has always been sacred to me. It is a very emotional/spiritual experience. Spiritual for me means there is a powerful connection. I wouldn't have sex with someone I wasn't emotionally touched by and didn't love. Sacred sexuality is expansive, synergistic. Together you create another reality that is different from the usual dimension. It is like creating a third dimension. Nancy

CONTEMPLATIVE SEX

In contemplative love there is no specific aim. There is nothing particular that has to happen.

Sit naked in meditation together. Do nothing to excite yourself or your partner. Don't fantasize or will anything to happen. Allow the mind to be free of expectations. Keep the senses and the mind open.

Bring attention to your own breathing. Allow the body and mind to quiet as the breath becomes the object of attention.

The focus of attention continues to be the breath. Allow the focus of attention to open out to include your partner. Breathing together you become aware of a circle of energy. Feel the circle of energy passing from one to the other. The warmth of the fire, the female fire infuses your body and the body of your partner.

Open the circle of energy to include yourself, your partner, and the space that you are in. Keep breathing and opening the focus of attention so the circle widens. Breathe, and as the breath deepens, allow it to encompass the whole of the Earth. Breathe with the earth. Feel the pulse of the Earth. Feel the beat of your heart, your partner's heart. As you breathe, any sense of separation dissolves. You are the breath. You are the wind. You are the fire. You are the Earth. Breathe.

THE HEALING POWER OF INTIMATE RELATIONSHIPS

Intimate relationships can open us to the pain that we have hidden from ourselves and others. When we honestly touch this pain, without denial or attachment, it is a sacred act. We are present to our experience, without trying to hide it or make it different than it is. The acceptance of all our feelings—the confusion, the doubt, the pain, the excitement, the longing, the heat, and the joy—can be transformative. There is no place we have to be to make our sex sacred. The sacredness is in our full presence in the moment.

My friend Cindy, an incest survivor, talked to me about how her meditation practice had a positive effect on her sexuality:

I started meditating during a time when sex was difficult for me because incest memories were surfacing. I had been getting upset and aggravated whenever the memories came up. This gave them more power. Then I began using the meditative approach of present moment awareness. When making love and having a memory, I asked myself, Is the abuse happening now or did it happen in the past? I turned my attention, gently, from the memories to the sensations in my body or to seeing myself or my partner or the room I was presently in. The memories came up less and less often.

What I did was a twofold process. First I noticed myself thinking thoughts like: Here comes another memory. It's going to destroy this whole evening. It is going to ruin my life. I'll never be able to have sex. I would see this mental process and say, oh, that's just a mental process. It isn't necessarily telling me the truth. I didn't spend much time with the fear because when I noticed the thinking, I would bring myself to what was real in the present moment, such as a hand touching my arm. Its realness was more compelling. Of course, I had to choose other times, when I wasn't making love, to stay with the memories themselves, giving them the attention they needed. If I hadn't also been doing that, I don't think I could have let them go during sex times.

I didn't practice meditation to get rid of the memories. Doing anything to rid myself of the memories always backfired. To this day I have to be open to knowing that memories will arise sometimes during sex. I still have them

but the frequency has been drastically reduced. My attitude now, many years later, is when memories come up, they come up. Sometimes it means I have to let go of making love and sometimes it doesn't. Sometimes the memories go away in a moment. The key is the openness to it.

After this period, meditation began to transform my sexuality in another way. I was meditating regularly and doing retreats. My meditations were body-focused. I did a lot of body sweeping, systematically becoming aware of all the different sensations in my body from my head to my toes and back again. I became very intimate with every crevice and cell in my body, all the tingling, all the pressures, all the sensations. My body became more alive because I woke up to it. I began to feel much more subtle levels of physical sensation. This meant I was feeling more subtle levels of discomfort as well as pleasure and neutrality. I began to have more physical sensation during sex. And a lot of sex is pleasurable sensations so this was a very welcome experience in my life.

I want to be more specific. I have always had orgasms. Because I am an incest survivor people are surprised to know that I have orgasms. But in the past it wasn't so enjoyable, it was just an explosion of energy. So when I say my pleasure increased, it's not that I started having orgasms, but that my whole body became alive. When someone touched me anywhere on my body in a sensual manner it felt pleasurable for the first time. I began to feel sensuality all over and to savor it. And my orgasms were affected, too, because all the sensations leading up to orgasm became intensely pleasurable. Orgasms became exciting and deep, and I had many more of them at a time. What happened for me with the body sweeping meditation was that my attention went fully to each physical sensation. Like now, feeling the wind on our faces. We can't fully experience the pleasure of that if our attention isn't fully open to it. I think that energy pathways in my body opened up.

PLEASURES

We both sat there, two disabled lesbians in our wheelchairs, each on opposite sides of the bed. Sudden feelings of fear and timidness came over us. But once we finished the transferring, lifting of legs, undressing and arranging of blankets, we finally touched. Softly and slowly we began to explore each other, our minds and bodies. Neither could make assumptions about the sensations or pleasures of the other. It was wonderful to sense that this woman felt that my body was worth the time it took to explore, that she was as interested in discovering my pleasure as I was in discovering hers.

From the first touch it was a stream of sensations: to listen to every breath, each sigh, and to feel every movement of our love intermingling. It was so intense, so mutual that I must say this beginning was one of the deepest and most fulfilling that I have ever experienced.

When I was an able–bodied lesbian, my approach to relating sexually had been to find out what moves turned someone on and go from there. Never before have I taken the time or had the opportunity to begin a relationship with such a beautiful feeling of pleasure, not only from the pot of gold at the end of the rainbow, but also from the exploration itself. Diane Hugs

SHOW ME THE PICTURES AGAIN

Show me the pictures again
The ones from before
When you were less disabled
But still a crip.
I want
To see them again.
Show me the ones
Where you're climbing the tree
And it takes me a minute to see
That you're doing it all with your arms.
Show me the one where you "fake" standing up
I want to see how tall you are,
And the one after that, when you fall
Into your lover's arms
And as you fall
You smile.

Your beautiful smile...
Your beautiful breasts...
The bare–breasted picture
Of you in your wheelchair
Wearing a hat and an open vest
You know, the one where I have to look
Really carefully
To see that your eyes are not focussed
To see that then you were blind.
Show me that picture again.

Show me the pictures before that
The ones when you were less paralyzed
The ones when you walked.
And speaking of walking...
I'm so worried I'll make a mistake
I've used "walking" and "numb"
As easy metaphors
As though everyone walked, really
As though no one was numb, really
I deepen my knowing
Of what's true, what's real
In the process I make mistakes.

Pictures do capture parts of the soul:
Your softness, your sweetness
Your courage
Your style:
Jauntily butch
Hat and vest
Your breasts...
Your smile...
Etheric residue
In the contact sheets
Show me the pictures
I want to see more

Barbara Ruth

JUDITH & TERRI

Judith

I feel it is a major accomplishment in my life to have reclaimed my sexuality. Recovering from sexual abuse is a great struggle for me and I am learning the things I need to relearn. With my sexuality I have come full circle. I feel strong and empowered sexually. There is a way in my relationship with Terri I have returned to parts of myself. It's been years since I have been in relationship with another fat woman and a woman close to my age. Terri and I have a similar class background and have connected on an impulsive, energetic level. Being with myself, being who I am, is a great gift.

Terri

I think in a relationship in general the struggles of paying the bills, going to work, dealing with children, take us away from each other. Being sexual is a way to pull closer together. If I'm feeling distant emotionally, sex can pull me back into the depth of my feeling. If there are things in my life that make me sad or I haven't been treated well, it can be healing to be with a lover who treats me with respect and tenderness. When I can feel the truth of her love it heals hurt places. It provides me with strength to deal with the vagaries of life. It is a source of sustenance.

The hard part is not the sexuality but the increased visibility in the world. As two fat women, we're more visible. I'm a large woman and Judith is larger than I am. So we get a lot of people's fatphobia. And knowing that things are more limited for her than for me in some ways, because she is larger, is difficult.

The first thing I noticed when I started being sexual with my lover was the sheer weight of her body on me. It was an exhilarating feeling. My other lovers had been smaller than me and they had talked to me about what it felt like to have the weight of my body against them. I had never experienced it myself. To feel Judith's weight as she lay against me was amazing.

The round, smooth softness of her body feels differently than someone who is small and you feel their bones and muscles. To feel a full fat woman who has lots of curves and flesh is a different feeling under your hands. It is very erotic for me. It has added to the appreciation of my own body because I love hers so much. It's made me feel what my body must feel like to her. It is very powerful to make love to someone who has a large body in the sense you are directing and controlling a body that is larger than yours. It is powerful and erotic to have power that someone is letting you have.

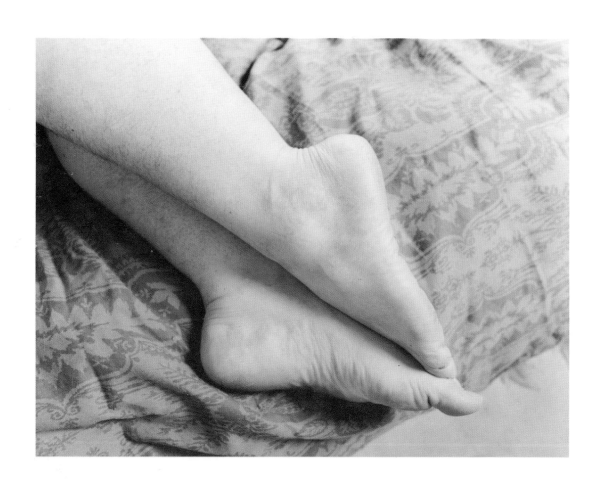

JOSH & KAREN

Josh

Sexuality with Karen is sacred to me, but sexuality and spiritual experiences in the past have been two different things for me. In my generation gays and lesbians were very closeted. When I came out, butch and femme were a big part of being a lesbian. I definitely identify as a butch. Sexually I felt more comfortable pleasuring my lover. That has dramatically changed in my relationship with Karen. Karen gives me a lot of gifts that have to do with her age: opening up sexually, opening up emotionally, a sense of playfulness. Her being uninhibited creates a safe space for my self–expression. I am able to be more vulnerable with her. I have no doubt this vulnerability will bring me more in touch with my emotions and allow me to be more receptive. I think in time my sexuality and my spirituality will merge into a oneness I have never experienced before.

Karen

The sexual experience is the most vulnerable moment. It is a gift, it is divine, an altered state. It overcomes my person. Making love is touching souls. Sacred sexuality is oneness with the universe. In my generation people are more open to sexuality as just who you are, less judgmental about roles. We bend more. Josh refers to the butch/femme thing, but people my age don't make that classification.

Karen: *Josh and I talked about making love in the Mustang. Cars are connected to guys being in control and girls being helpless. Girls lose their virginity in the back seats of cars, so our being photographed in the Mustang is taking back our power. After all, the Mustang is a woman's car. I identify it totally with my sexuality. It's letting go, being primitive. It is raw freedom.*

Josh: *The Mustang symbolizes freedom and power to me, also. The Mustang isn't just a car; it's a beautiful work of art, a sculpture on wheels. This car was an American icon when it was built, and it's still an American icon thirty years later. Karen was not even born when this car was built.*

SO STILL THE DAWN

Two in collusion
Plotting—simply—pleasure,
A playing together.

We could not know it for the time
The loin's explosion would beget
Volcanoes.

So still the dawn
Quivering at the rim of day:
Your waking touch invading
Dreams.

Sleep co–conspirator:
No sentry at love's
Gate.

Gentle, gentle
The double kiss:
Mouth vulva open

In mutual bliss
Each into each
Merging.

Dawn's furnace reddens;
The blood's drums mutter.
Enthused
No long self–possessing,
As Maenads of Bacchus, we
Possessed.

Enter, O, enter
The inmost holy place;
At the altar, self–anointing
And anointed, dance
Your dance.

Till flesh, transfused
With burning breath becomes
Veil of the Goddess; and
Earth heaves.

The fiery lava floods;
We whirl with the stars,
No cell of self un–
Exploded.

Elsa Gidlow, 1967

letters to kate

*that it is sacred. body curves into rock curves into body ancient cold
radiates up vertebrae the body shivers is held the stone walls rise up,
succulents the color of sea foam cling to them. somewhere in the canyon bees
hum mantram of the world beginning there is no other sound. yr smell.
hawk skims the air just above our heads our shoes dry in the sun. later we
climb an old slide spread our bodies open to winter light but the shiver does
not stop.*

*we lie in warm sand circled by boulders listening to the creek slide past.
head nestles in breast arms legs around & through. nothing moves but the
heart. this peace new and familiar this fire. membranes dissolve. and
galaxies star systems yr mouth finds mine we go down to rise again the
constellations exhale. to enter once more the still center as shadows spread
across pale stone.*

Joan Iten Sutherland

WOMAN FOREVER

I have always wanted to be both man and woman, to incorporate the strongest and richest parts of my mother and father within/into me—to share valleys and mountains upon my body the way the earth does in hills and peaks.

I would like to enter a woman the way any man can, and to be entered—to leave and to be left—to be hot and hard and soft all at the same time in the cause of our loving. I would like to drive forward and at other times to rest or be driven. When I sit and play in the waters of my bath I love to feel the deep inside parts of me, sliding and folded and tender and deep. Other times I like to fantasize the core of it, my pearl, a protruding part of me, hard and sensitive and vulnerable in a different way.

I have felt the age–old triangle of mother father and child, with the "I" at its eternal core, elongate and flatten out into the elegantly strong triad of grandmother mother daughter, with the "I" moving back and forth flowing in either or both directions as needed.

Woman forever. My body, a living representation of other life older longer wiser. The mountains and valleys, trees, rocks. Sand and flowers and water and stone. Made in earth. Audre Lorde

O Honeysuckle Woman

won't you lay with me
our tongues flowering
open–throated
golden pollen
We could drink one another
sticky sweet & deep
our bodies tracing silver snail trails
Our white teeth nibbling
We could swallow desire whole
fingers caught in our sweet smell
We'd transform the air
O honey woman
won't you suckle me
Suckling
won't you let me
honey you

Chrystos

smooth brown skin

i love to touch smooth brown skin and run my fingers through grey flecked hair feeling the different movements and textures as my hands course over your body experiencing the different reactions i receive for my touch i'm afraid of losing myself in you oh i need love to be such a struggle i think not now that i have chosen to love you and feel you now i'm afraid i'll die before i get the chance to taste all of what we have to offer each other these feelings run through my mind as my hands are touring your back your face feeling and seeing are what hands do i can shut my eyes and drink you in seeing the golden tones of your flesh your essence feeling the warmth that exudes from yourself to my hands to me watching as you change as i change i find i like brown skin more and more and more it is likened to a reflection of myself and at times we touch it is not unlike touching myself touching makes me realize how important my hands are being reminded of sensations so far apart yet so close i think of you and i weave and the sun is reflected off my back and i am immersed in color and texture and am reminded of how it is after making love to you and we lie together with the sun reflecting over both our brown bodies and watch how they glisten as we breathe and move and move closer to each other to begin again brown skin is what i'm working with grey flecked hair like silk is what i touch caress pull move from your face to behind your ear brown skin that is golden and smooth soft and hard all at the same time like the warp on my loom waiting to be manipulated and caressed by skillful gentle hands weaving the colors blending them together

Berjé A. Barrow

BERJÉ & JOSEPHINA

Berjé

I believe that sacredness encompasses everything in one's life and that sexuality also encompasses everything in one's life. We don't get to be sexual or spiritual if we don't go through some tribulations. Tribulation is when you go inside and face the shadow. Each time I do I come back stronger, softer, more understanding and more forgiving of myself. We are sexual beings. It is one of the biggest crimes of our culture that we are forced to deny who we are as women, who we are as lesbians, who we are as women of color. Historically women of color have been treated either as old dykes or as sultry, sexy (not sexual) creatures. And being thought of as creatures, we are thought of as not human, and we can be taken advantage of and abused.

I can have a sacred sexual experience by myself, walking down the street. Sacred sexuality is about how I allow myself to be. One of the best sacred sexual experiences I had was with a friend. We treated ourselves to a sushi bar where we ate for two hours and then we went dancing. We never once sat down. We danced until the place closed. I get into tribal dancing. Everyone thinks you have to be cool on the dance floor. No, you have to be wild, wicked, open and out–there. On that dance floor I experienced the spiritual ecstacy you get when you let go. I believe it's what women do in the forests of South America or on the plains of Africa. It was energizing, awesome, inspiring. It was an orgasmic experience and no one even touched me. It was as if my friend and I danced with everyone on the dance floor and then transcended it. We were rising above without leaving the ground. You don't have to die to go to heaven. You can get it now. I have moments of it. I don't go into a blank space but it is space.

I can go into that space with a partner when we're being physical and experiencing all the nuances of our own bodies. I can also do it when I walk into a room where there are people that I love. It is only momentary but it is teaching me to be appreciative and savor the encounters. It is wholeness. Each moment in my life has gotten me to this point where I can understand, accept and wholly take in all that has occurred. I am learning to stay open and celebrate. When I was younger sex was magical: Oh, my body can really do these interesting things. Now it is mystical. It moves from magical to mystical when the divine has entered it. When I as lesbian realize that sex is a holy act, there is a vibrant, mystical quality.

Being lovers with another woman of color opened the door to reclaiming my identity. Once I was lying in bed talking with my lover, my arm was across her chest and I thought—we match. It wasn't just matching color wise. It was about melting and merging. I had an awareness of being with all my senses. There was contour, there was shadow. I got to see the texture of my skin. I could see, hear, taste and smell the colors our bodies created.

HOW DOES THIS BODY WANT TO BE TOUCHED?

How does this body want to move? How does this body want to respond? Invite pleasure. Touch lightly, letting fingers run over flesh barely touching the skin, like the brush of a feather. Touch firmly, surely. Vary pressures. Make circles, open out moving slowly, and follow the pulse, increasing the speed as pulse quickens. Tease, pull back. Press lightly, more insistently. Use palms and fingers, squeeze, pinch. Notice the skin, cool, warm, moist or dry. Let yourself fully appreciate the changes in skin texture. Find the most sensitive places. Adore them. Play with mouths. Licking, sucking, biting. Let the tongue trail over the body. Open to all the pleasures of smell, drink in the aroma of sex, breathe into all the damp, moist places. Inhale the scent of your lover. Embrace the feelings that are aroused, the thoughts that dance within the mind. Let the thoughts dance freely. Invite the intimacy of the breath. Breathe together. Let the wind play with you. Watch all the ways the breath touches you. Inside and out. Invite color and sound. Sing the praises of the body. Seek ways to open to the body beyond the physical body, to the senses beyond the physical senses. Rejoice.

LET ME TOUCH

like falling cherry petals your face
after you come circling in the stillness
our hearts like hummingbirds
let me sweet pink & tender kiss your breasts
your eyes closed softly in dreams of whirling stars
our bellies
wet & stuck

Chrystos

SPIRITUAL LOVE

The deepest yearning in the human heart is for love, for union with the Beloved. We seek to merge, to awaken to Oneness with the Goddess or the whole of creation. This search is the essence of all spiritual and mystical traditions. In mystical or spiritual love, there is no love object. Love is warm, caring, kind attention given without expectation of any return. Expectations only lead to disappointment. When we have expectations, we aren't able to receive what is there. We are too focused on what we want to be there. Learning to give without expecting anything in return may seem unrealistic. The miracle of love is that it moves in a circle so that, when we give love in an open–hearted way, it does come back to us.

Eros, love, our erotic knowledge is our passionate connection to life. When we are vibrant and awake, deeply connected to the source of creation, this informs everything we see. The world appears fresh and new when seen through the eyes of love. There is beauty even within deep suffering because the world is sparkling with aliveness. We are able to take in the whole of life, all the pains and all the joys. Body of woman, body of lesbian, body of love, body of wisdom, body of body, body of Earth, is sacred.

THE CHARGE OF THE GODDESS

I who am the beauty of the green earth and the white moon among the stars, and the mysteries of the waters, and the Desire in the Heart of Woman, I call upon your soul to arise and come unto me. For I am the soul of nature that gives life to the universe. From Me all things proceed and unto Me they must return. Let My worship be in the heart that rejoices, for behold—all acts of love and pleasure are My rituals. Let there be beauty and strength, power and compassion, honor and humility, mirth and reverence within you. And you who seek to know Me, know that your seeking and yearning will avail you not, unless you know the Mystery: for if that which you seek, you find not within yourself, you will never find it without. For behold, I have been with you from the beginning, and I am that which is attained at the end of desire.

Traditional, adapted from Starhawk and Doreen Valiente

IN THE BLAZE OF LOVE

In the blaze of love it is known:
We are particles each of each
We are cells of the Mother of all
We cannot be cast off
From sister cells or from Her.

Her breath is the breath of our lungs
Her heart beat times our own;
Where She is winged we fly,
We swim with Her dolphins; wind
through rocks with Her jeweled snakes;
We bloom in Her million flowers;
We grow in Her ancient trees
And die in a night with Her moths.

In rock we wait with Her
Dreaming of fin or flesh,
Of the awful miracle
Of human heart and mind.

In the blaze of love it is known,
No being, no life is born,
Exists, or dies alone.

Elsa Gidlow, 1975

SOURCE NOTES

❦ Page xiii: "...Inanna's descent to the underworld": "Celebrated for 3500 years, Inanna was the most important deity in Sumerian mythology. Originally a Goddess of the Earth and fertility, she appears in some of the most erotic poetry ever written. ... The story of Inanna's descent tells how she, the Queen of Heaven, decides to go visit her sister Ereshkigal, the Queen of the Underworld. ... (S)he sets off alone and passes through the seven gates to the underworld. She must give up a symbol of her power (her crown, staff, various jewels, and robe) at each. ... Inanna's is the oldest tale we have of the journey of death and rebirth. It precedes and influences the stories of Persephone, Orpheus, and Jesus by millennia." Hallie Iglehart Austen, *The Heart of the Goddess*. Berkeley, CA: Wingbow Press, 1990, p. 74.

❦ Page 1:   "Invocation to Sappho:" Elsa Gidlow, *Sapphic Songs*. Mill Valley, CA: Druid Heights Books, 1982, p. 1.

❦ Page 5:   "The female power of the serpent..." Sandy Boucher, "Meeting the Tiger," originally published in *Snake Power*, Vol. 1, Issue 1.

❦ Page 16:   "Sometimes now I watch younger people..." Ibid.

❦ Page 31:   "Because we are obsessed with sex..." Ibid.

❦ Page 35:   "... And my responses have changed..." Ibid.

❦ Page 45:   "A lesbian woman is drawn to a union..." Karin Lofthus Carrington, "Women Loving Women: Speaking the Truth in Love," in Hopcke, Carrington and Wirth, eds., *Same-Sex Love and the Path to Wholeness*. Boston: Shambhala, 1993, p. 95.

❦ Page 76:   "There were green plantains..." Audre Lorde, *Zami: A New Spelling of My Name*. Freedom, CA: Crossing Press, 1982, p. 249.

❦ Page 85:   "...the beloved does not attempt to control..." Judy Grahn, *Another Mother Tongue*. Boston: Beacon Press, 1984, p. 255.

❦ Page 85:   Ibid., p. 256.

❦ Page 85:   Ibid., p. 257.

❦ Page 103:   Lorde, *Zami*, p. 7.

❦ Page 112:   Traditional, version here by Starhawk, *The Spiral Dance*. San Francisco: HarperCollins, 1989, pp. 90-91, and by Doreen Valiente, English Witch.

❦ Page 115:   Unpublished poem from the Elsa Gidlow Estate.

BIBLIOGRAPHY

Austen, Hallie Iglehart. *The Heart of the Goddess: Art, Myth and Meditations of the World's Sacred Feminine*. Berkeley, CA: Wingbow Press, 1990.

Boucher, Sandy. "Meeting the Tiger," in Noble, ed., *Snake Power*, Vol. 1, Issue 1.

Carrington, Karin Lofthus. "Women Loving Women: Speaking the Truth in Love." In Hopcke, Carrington and Wirth, eds., *Same-Sex Love and the Path to Wholeness*. Boston: Shambhala, 1993.

Chrystos. *Not Vanishing*. Vancouver, Canada: Press Gang Publishers, 1988.

Gidlow, Elsa. *Sapphic Songs: Eighteen to Eighty*. Mill Valley, CA: Druid Heights Books, 1982.

Grahn, Judy. *Another Mother Tongue*. Boston: Beacon Press, 1984.

Lorde, Audre. *Zami: A New Spelling of My Name*. Freedom, CA: Crossing Press, 1982.

Noble, Vicki, ed. *Snake Power*. Berkeley, CA: Snake Power, 1989.

Ruth, Barbara. *Past, Present and Future Passions*. Santa Cruz, CA: Her Books, 1986.

Silvermarie, Sue. *Menopausal Lust*. Milwaukee, WI: Silvermarie Productions.

Starhawk. *The Spiral Dance*. San Francisco: HarperCollins, 1989.

ACKNOWLEDGEMENTS

The energy, care, love and input of many women have made this book possible. The wondrous, strong lesbian women I wish to acknowledge here are not listed in the order of their importance. We are a circle. First, thank you Marcelina for inviting me to write the text to accompany your marvelous photographs. Patti Levy, you were also fully present along this journey, being photographed, printing the pictures, reading rough drafts, and sharing your intimate experiences; I'm most appreciative. I'm thankful for all the conversations I had with the women who were photographed, especially those I didn't meet in person, who were willing to speak over the phone about the most sacred, intimate parts of their lives. How lesbian of you! And to each of the women photographed, may the power of your courage be witness to the strength of us all. Sandy Boucher read a few first paragraphs and suggested I interview the women whose photographs would be used. The story "Initiation" was written in the women's spiritual journey writing group she facilitates. Sandy, I appreciate your steadfast support of my writing since we first met shortly after I moved to the West Coast. Barbara Ruth, you listened and edited from the beginning; always I felt your support and am grateful for your insight. Barbara Waugh, Stacy Cusulos, Linda Moakes, Candice Chace, Annie Hershey, Carol Newhouse, and Arachne Stevens, I am grateful for all your love, support, humor, and insights. Thanks to Arinna Weisman for clarifications of the dharma. To Barbara Zoloth my gratitude and devotion for being a computer consultant as well as the designated driver and giving editorial assistance. Sue Silvermarie—our stories go back to Cambridge in the Seventies and I remain in awe of your poetic spirit and am honored to share your poems. And to each of the poets, I am honored that your work will grace this book. My sons Jake and Mike Flaherty have been enthusiastic and supportive as always. Jake has offered emotional and artistic support from the beginning. His calm explanation of the workings of a computer have saved the day on many occasions. Mike returned to the West Coast as the final edits were in process. He read some of the manuscript and his humor often served to get me back on track. Finally to my editors at Wingbow: Randy, thanks for holding the vision with kindness and clarity; André, I'm so happy you met Marcelina in line waiting for the Tenth Anniversary celebration of Good Vibrations; working with you has been delightful.

Diane Mariechild

Acknowledgements for the birth of a project like this start at the beginning. My roots were put down early and deep in the richness of the Georgia Coastal Plains. My grandmother anchored me close to the Sacredness of the Earth. My parents told me that I could be anything I wanted, and I believed them. Their strength of character and intense individualism required me to find my truest self. Learning to thank them is an ongoing process.

To Judy Allen, who expanded my sense of reality from a small Georgia town to a world that reached through centuries and continents, I give eternal applause. For more than new horizons, she pointed my soul towards the possibility of sacred love. Just her presence widened my dreams and opened my heart. How can I bow deeply enough to the woman who set me on my life's path?

A long line of friendships and loves has graced my life. For the many people who have shown me the art of living, I tip my hat. Their belief in my art with unwavering encouragement and support kept me moving through my own doubt. I want to extend a special gratitude to all those people, particularly to Hallie Iglehart Austen, Greg Day, Gay Dellinger, Ruth Eckland, Vicki Gabriner, Elsa Gidlow, Elizabeth Min, Celeste West, and Irene Young.

In undertaking this book, I met the most demanding challenge I have faced as an artist. Diane waded into deep, sometimes rushing waters with me and still managed to find ground in the end. An ongoing gratitude to you, Diane, for accepting such a challenging project. Energy rushed in unpredictably to keep this project moving at various times when I thought I had lost the thread. Irene Young was more than generous with her time and her studio. Greg Day, my coyote muse since college, provided humor and insight into the sisterhood. His French Renaissance bedroom was a perfect setting; I will always think of San Francisco from that particular window. The classical labyrinth in the last photograph was beautifully reconstructed by Hallie Iglehart Austen and Gwen Jones and provided an image to punctuate the spirit in which the whole project was undertaken. I clap my hands wildly to Arisika Razak for her perfect embodiment of the Goddess. Celeste West in her infinite brilliance spun gold and stars around my shoulders when the fog descended. Kit Weiler was the acid test for the initial sequencing of the images. Judy Allen gave me the key to the introduction and reminded me once again to take my own path. Hallie Iglehart Austen walked the entire path with me from start to finish. Her friendship goes beyond all beginnings and endings.

A more distantly related but vitally important circle was the group of people who gave me ballast at various times through these three years. Greg Schelkun so graciously kept me afloat during the worst part of my illness and never allowed me to forget that creativity was my real place in this world. Becca Barnett managed to steer me through my dark night without losing the tow rope in high seas. I will always send silent prayers in your direction. Susun Weed dreamed me well and ushered in the High Priestess. Natalie Goldberg's work drew me out of a few stuck places when I simply *had* to move on.

To all those involved directly with the production of this book a warm thanks. To my printer, friend, and kindred spirit, Patti Levy, I owe much. Her expertise as a printer gave my vision form. Her constant willingness to be there for any artistic advice and help cannot be underestimated. She was the midwife. Joan Iten Sutherland guided me almost every step of the book with her nonpareil insight. Her editorial wisdom more than once has brightened women's books. She polished our stone in unaccounted for ways. Randy Fingland, you are much appreciated. Your strong vision of a harmonious world sends a lot of art into the world that otherwise might be seen by few. A hearty thanks goes to André for introducing *Lesbian Sacred Sexuality* to Wingbow with such great gusto. Her perseverance and wholehearted efforts were instrumental in bringing the work to print. Denice Dearing's design of the book brought simple elegance to a complex project.

To the women who allowed their images to be recorded, I have the greatest gratitude and respect. It is through your courage and honesty that this book is possible. Without you, there could be no *Lesbian Sacred Sexuality*. I hope your generosity of spirit returns a thousandfold. You touched my heart and will touch the hearts of many, many more through your openness.

Finally, a great gassho to Oralani Fuller, a partner who never failed to give strength, nourishment, and hope when there was none. Your gentle calls to the frontline were integral to my fine tuning the images. Burma-Roshi and you bring deep peace, reminding me that there really is unconditional love on Earth. Wild Hearts Ranch brings my life full circle. I am anchored once again to our sacred Earth.

Marcelina Martin

ABOUT THE AUTHOR AND PHOTOGRAPHER

Barbara Zoloth © 1994

Diane Mariechild

Diane Mariechild is a student of Ruth Denison, and has studied with Buddhist teachers in both Theravadan and Vajrayana traditions; she has taught in Dhyani Ywahoo's Peacekeeper Training Program and is a teacher of vipassana meditation. Ms. Mariechild is the mother of two grown sons and lives with her partner in northern California. She is the author of *Mother Wit* and *The Inner Dance*, both from Crossing Press, as well as *Open Mind: Women's Daily Inspiration for Becoming Mindful*, from HarperSanFrancisco.

Karen Pabst © 1994

Marcelina Martin

Marcelina Martin became a photographer in the South in 1963. Since 1979, she has lived in the San Francisco Bay Area. Her photography has been published in such books as *Southern Ethic, Women See Woman, Womanspirit: A Guide to Women's Wisdom, Women & Aging, Elsa: I Come With My Songs, The Womanspirit Sourcebook, The Once and Future Goddess, The Heart of the Goddess* and *The Box: Remembering the Gift*. Her prints have been exhibited in Australia, Germany, Denmark, and throughout the United States. Ms. Martin's work is also included in the Women's History Archives Collection at Harvard University and in the Brown University Visual Art Slide Library. Currently, she is working on a series of Polaroid transfers in northern New Mexico entitled *She-Stallion of the High Desert: Horses and the Untamed Feminine*. For information and a brochure regarding Ms. Martin's photography, send an SASE to
Wild Hearts Ranch, PO Box 2886, Taos, NM 87571.